MY ANCE
WAS AN APPRENTICE

HOW CAN I FIND OUT MORE ABOUT HIM?

by Stuart A. Raymond

SOCIETY OF GENEALOGISTS ENTERPRISES LTD

Published by

Society of Genealogists Enterprises Limited
14 Charterhouse Buildings, Goswell Road
London EC1M 7BA

© The Society of Genealogists Enterprises and the author 2010.

ISBN: 978-1-907199-03-5

British Library Cataloguing in Publication Data.
A CIP Catalogue record for this book is available from the British Library

The Society of Genealogists Enterprises Limited is a wholly owned subsidiary of the Society of Genealogists, a registered charity, no 233701

Acknowledgements

This book could not have been written without the aid of the many books which are listed in the bibliography and footnotes. I hope that due acknowledgement has been made where appropriate. I must also thank Cliff Webb and Else Churchill, who checked my text and shared their knowledge of apprenticeship records with me. The remaining errors, I am afraid, are mine.

Stuart A. Raymond

About the Author

Stuart Raymond studied history and politics at Keele University, and submitted a thesis based on Cornish probate records for his Adelaide University MA. He also studied librarianship at the College of Librarianship Wales. After a spell as librarian of the Yorkshire Archaeological Society in the late 1970s, he spent many years as an academic librarian in Australia, before returning to the UK in 1990. Since then, his publications have included numerous genealogical bibliographies, directories of genealogical websites, and other handbooks for family and local historians. Stuart is currently one of the partners of the Family History Partnership, who recently published his *The Census 1801-1911: a guide for the internet era (*2009) and *Parish registers: a history and guide* (2009). He is currently working on a guide to occupational sources for family historians.

www.stuartraymond.co.uk

CONTENTS

ILLUSTRATIONS

1. Tuckers Hall, Exeter, home of Exeter's Incorporation of Weavers, Tuckers & Shearmen (p.27).

2. Apprenticeship Indenture for Thomas Cape, 1721. Reproduced by permission of Exeter City Council (p.33).

3. Page of abstracts from Apprentices of Great Britain 1710-1774. **www.originsnetwork.com/help/aboutbo-appgb.aspx** (p.50).

4. The entry for Chas Paget (see illus 3) in London Apprenticeship Abstracts 1442-1850. **www.originsnetwork.com/help/aboutbo-lonapps.aspx** (p.51).

5. Apprenticeship indenture for Charles Paget, held in the Crisp & Clench collection by the Society of Genealogists (p.52).

Cover illustration

Industry and Idleness is one of the memorable engravings that English painter William Hogarth brought to this world. A full description of all twelve plates in the series which results in the 'idle prentice' executed at Tyburn and the 'industrious prentice' created Lord Mayor of London can be found online at **http://en.wikipedia.org/wiki/ Industry_and_Idleness** However the description of this first plate is worth quoting here:

Credited with pioneering western sequential art, his works are normally aimed at ridiculing the local norms, customs and politics. In Industry and Idleness, Hogarth brought to light the story of two apprentices in twelve plot-linked engravings.

In plate 1, The Fellow 'Prentices at their Looms', the two protagonists are introduced: both are 'prentices' on equal terms with their master, and doing the same work. The two characters rigorously follow their respective traits: Francis is busy at work with his loom and shuttle, with his copy of 'The Prentice's Guide' at his feet, and various wholesome literature tacked up on the wall behind him such as 'The London Prentice' and (portentously) 'Whitington Ld Mayor'.

Tom Idle leans snoring against his still loom, probably as a result of a huge mug labeled 'Spittle Fields' sitting on his loom. A clay pipe is wedged into the handle and a cat is busy fooling with the shuttle. Tacked to the post he's sleeping against is 'Moll Flanders'; his 'Prentice's Guide' is also lying on the ground, but in a completely filthy and shredded state.

To the right, their master looks disappointedly at Thomas, with a thick stick in his left hand.

Their future courses are marked off for them by the imagery surrounding the frame of the painting: to the left, representing Idle's future, a whip, fetters and a rope; to the right, over Goodchild, a ceremonial mace, sword of state and golden chain. The master's sword segues exactly into the shaft of the mace: more foreshadowing for the second encounter of the two in plate 10.

Idle's verse:
Proverbs: 23 v.21
'The Drunkard shall come to Poverty, & drowsiness shall
cloath a Man wth rags'
Goodchild's: Proverbs: 10 v.4
'The hand of the diligent maketh rich'.

CHAPTER ONE

Introduction

We all have apprentices amongst our ancestors. For several centuries, it was a legal requirement to serve an apprenticeship before practicing a trade. Many of our ancestors complied with this requirement. Apprenticeship indentures and registers, freemen's registers and a variety of other sources record their compliance. These records deserve more attention from family historians than they have received. They are particularly useful for the period between c.1550 and 1850, although some earlier and some later records can also be found. The aim of this book is to outline the history of apprenticeship, to describe the records which survive and to suggest ways in which family historians may investigate their ancestral apprentices.

The origins of apprenticeship are lost in the mists of history, but it is probable that it began in twelfth- and thirteenth-century London. The prime feature of apprenticeship as it was practised in medieval London was the residence of the apprentice in his master's household, for a minimum term of seven years. Of almost equal importance was the use of indentures which set out the behaviour expected from both master and apprentice. These indentures were enrolled in the city's records, and were legally binding. Guilds and the city authorities concerned themselves with the administration of apprenticeship, making a variety of regulations.

Enrolment, for example, was first ordered in 1230[1]. Only householders could be masters. They were normally men, although it was possible to be apprenticed to a woman. Widows who continued their husband's trades might keep on their husband's apprentices, or might 'turn them over' to another master.

London's example was widely followed. The 'custom of London' is mentioned in Bridgewater in 1424[2], and in Bristol in the late fifteenth century[3]. It was accepted as the national standard by the Statute of Artificers in 1563.

The essence of apprenticeship was the provision of labour in exchange for training. The apprentice, represented by his parents or other sponsors, contracted with a master to learn his trade or craft. The master recruited one or two apprentices in order, in time, to secure trained assistance in his work. By the sixteenth century, many apprentices paid their master a premium, intended to cover costs until they learnt to be productive. They normally lived in their masters' households, as pre-industrial trades and crafts were usually practised in the home.

In the late eighteenth century, residence ceased to be expected of all apprentices. The employment of large numbers in factories made residence in the master's household both impractical, and, from the master's point of view, undesirable. The introduction of the factory system marked the beginning of the end for the traditional system of apprenticeship.

In the medieval period, apprentices were only found in towns and cities, such as London, Norwich, Bristol and York. The rise of apprenticeship was associated with the growth of trade guilds and livery companies. The terms 'guilds' and 'companies' were frequently used synonymously. Livery companies were London guilds whose officers wore a distinctive 'livery'.

Guilds were originally voluntary organisations, but they gradually acquired monopolistic powers from the crown, evidenced by their charters. They should not be confused with religious fraternities, although, prior to the Reformation, their functions sometimes overlapped. Guilds were concerned to ensure that the quality of workmanship in their trade was maintained, and to prevent excessive competition from throwing their members out of work. They therefore sought to regulate the relationship between master and apprentice, to prevent individual masters from taking too many apprentices, and to determine who could become an apprentice.

Guilds joined with each other to obtain the right to municipal self-government in their towns and cities. Through their guilds, tradesmen and craftsmen were able to claim the 'freedom' of their cities, giving them trading privileges, exemption from certain levies, and in some cases the right to vote for local officers and members of parliament. Apprenticeship to a freeman carried with it the right to the status of a freeman on the satisfactory conclusion of the term.

In the medieval period, apprentices were recruited from the 'best' families, who owned a moderate amount of property. In contrast to servants and labourers, they could aspire to become master craftsmen themselves, to have their own households, and to take on their own apprentices. Statutes of 1388/9 and 1405/6 banned the children of rural labourers from apprenticeship. The Black Death had caused a shortage of labourers, and parliaments dominated by manorial lords were anxious to prevent their villeins migrating to the towns. The effectiveness of this legislation may be judged by the fact that the citizens of London thought it necessary to seek exemption from it in 1429. The citizens of Oxford similarly sought exemption, but they twice failed in their petitions to get it[4].

By the mid-sixteenth century, shortage of labour had ceased to be a problem. Population was rising, and with it the number of unemployed. The dissolution of the monasteries removed the major institution which had offered poor relief, and the threatened hordes of young beggars were greatly feared by the ruling classes. They had to be controlled. Apprenticeship had always offered a means of social control over adolescent males, who were viewed as the most disruptive element in society. Elizabethan legislators extended its scope to cover the poorest classes. In 1563, the Statute of Artificers adapted the institution to cover rural labourers. In 1597 and 1601, the power to bind poor children as apprentices was given to parish officers.

Apprenticeship was governed for 251 years by the Statute of Artificers and Apprentices. It gave substantial householders the power to require anyone 'to be an apprentice and to serve in husbandry or in any other kind of art, mystery or science'. Everyone was expected to serve a minimum term of seven years as an apprentice. In theory, no-one was allowed to practice a trade unless he had served an apprenticeship. Mayors and Justices of the Peace were given the power of enforcement, and could intervene if either master or apprentice had complaint against each other. The 'custom of London' was to be observed. In theory, that included the registration of indentures. In practice, no provision for registration in country districts was made. Indentures were only enrolled where guilds and borough authorities made their own arrangements and insisted on enrolment. Outside of the boroughs, indentures were rarely enrolled and rural apprentices (other than paupers) are usually difficult to find. The records kept by boroughs, where they survive, make it possible to trace urban apprentices more easily. Indentures, apprenticeship registers, and freemen's registers, can all be found in county and borough record offices[5]. If there is no borough record offices, borough records are likely to be in the local county record office.

The law was not universally enforced, but it is probable that we all have ancestors who served an apprenticeship. In 1550, 11% of London's population were apprentices[6], in seventeenth century Gloucester, about 6%, in Bristol, 10%[7].

Responsibility for poor relief was given to parish overseers and churchwardens by acts of 1597 and 1601[8]. They were empowered to apprentice pauper children, who could be an enormous drain on parish finances. Parish officers used their powers of binding extensively. In particular, most bastard children were apprenticed.

Girls were apprenticed as well as boys. Hitherto, there had been very few female apprentices, but overseers had as much responsibility for girls as they had for boys. Many girls were apprenticed to widows to learn 'housewifery'. Perhaps a third of pauper apprentices were girls[9].

The extension of apprenticeship to paupers was a perversion of the medieval ideal of apprenticeship. These apprentices were not wanted by their masters, who frequently gave them little training. The work that they did gave them limited subsequent prospects. An institution that had provided good training for a minority of respectable adolescents became the parish overseer's solution to social problems that he was quite incapable of solving[10]. The recruitment of young apprentices for the factories of the north meant that the 'custom of London' ceased to be operative for these children, since one of its most important components - residence in the master's household - ceased to apply. Instead, separate houses were built specifically to house apprentices. Emscote Mill in 1782 had a 'new building ... as a house for apprentices'[11].

Parish apprenticeship exacerbated the tensions between master and apprentice, since many masters did not want paupers in their house. Indentures considerably reduced the personal freedom of young men. Apprentices were not allowed to visit alehouses, play cards, attend playhouses, or even leave their master's house without his permission. They could not commit fornication, nor were they allowed to marry during their apprenticeship. They had little, if any, money to spend. It is not surprising that many young men rebelled against such restrictions. Many absconded. From the late eighteenth century, newspapers frequently carried advertisements seeking the return of absconders. For example, in January 1812, an advertisement was placed in the *Times* seeking the return of James Gower, apprentice to Henry White, brush-maker, of Clerkenwell. A detailed description was given, and he was assured of good treatment when he returned - but anyone who employed him was threatened with the law. The records of Quarter Sessions and other courts are full of masters' complaints against their apprentices. There are not so many complaints of apprentices against their masters, but that is probably due to the fact that the system was weighted against them. The terms of their indentures were harsh. It is likely that, for many apprentices, absconding was easier than making an official complaint.

Apprenticeship was intended to offer a worthwhile training. Apprentices learnt their master's trade, lived in their master's household, and had a marketable skill at the end of their apprenticeship. They might also acquire social skills which would help them to rise in society, especially if they came from a lower station in life than their masters. Apprentices had security, and their training could provide the basis for future prosperity. Most mayors and aldermen of English towns and cities prior to the industrial revolution had served apprenticeships. In London, some 8% of early seventeenth-century aldermen had been apprentices who had married their masters' daughters[12].

A good apprenticeship offered scope for the ambitious son of an artisan. It also offered succour to those moving down the social scale. The younger sons of the gentry, and the children of clergy, sometimes needed a trade to support themselves. Orphans of the upper classes may have had to reduce their aspirations and to accept apprenticeship in a humbler station than their parents had occupied. They were frequently required by economic necessity to become merchants or surgeons, lawyers or manufacturers. During the seventeenth and eighteenth centuries, an increasingly large proportion of apprentices came from gentle families, who were able to pay substantial premiums and gradually monopolized the luxury trades[13].

The relationship between master and servant was close. Legally, the master stood *in loco parentis* to the apprentice. He usually had the responsibility of providing housing, clothing and food. He was expected to provide the training and experience that the apprentice needed before he could carry on his calling independently. He also had the responsibility for ensuring that his apprentices conformed to society's social and moral mores. In particular, he was expected to instil into them respect for authority and self-control.

The apprentice also had responsibilities. These were set out in indentures. As already noted, they were very restrictive of personal liberty. Many restrictions are laid down in the indentures printed below[14]. The apprentice's task was to learn, and to be obedient to his master. As he learnt, he would become more proficient and hence more useful to his master. If he was disobedient, his master was entitled, indeed expected, to exercise moderate discipline. That discipline was stern by modern standards. It sometimes led to retaliation from the apprentice, which may be recorded in court proceedings or newspapers. It was, however, limited. The master could not simply dismiss an unsatisfactory apprentice. That required the approval of Justices of the Peace. The misbehaviour or absence of an apprentice were grounds for cancellation of his indentures. Records of cancellations made by magistrates can frequently be found in apprenticeship registers and court records. For example, the indentures of John Watts, apprentice to Richard Aldridge of Oxford, were cancelled, 'on complaint of master'[15]. If the master suffered loss or damage as a result of his apprentice's misbehaviour, he could sometimes claim compensation from the apprentice's sponsor.

Apprentices rarely had any choice in the trade they were to learn, or in the master who would teach them. For parents, long-term security was the priority. They wanted their children to follow trades in which work was likely to be available throughout their lives, and which could provide a sufficient income to support them properly. Apprentices' destiny was determined by parental connections, or by the premium that they were able to pay. If parents were poor, the whim of the parish overseer, or support from some charitable organization, might be the determining factor. London masters, many of whom were migrants, frequently recruited their apprentices from their home villages.

Tradesmen sometimes apprenticed their children to others in the same trade. Between 1600 and 1800, the proportion of sons of freemen who entered their fathers' companies increased markedly[16]. In Sheffield, 35% of apprentices in the Cutlers Company were the sons of members of the Company[17]. This practice was less prevalent in Surrey, where surprisingly few apprentices followed their father's trade[18]. It may, of course, be that sons who took over their fathers' businesses were not always formally apprenticed. If their fathers were freemen, they could usually claim the freedom, that is, the right to trade, by patrimony, and may not have needed a formal apprenticeship. Nevertheless, some fathers did take their own sons as apprentices. In eighteenth century Oxford, the masters of 12.6% of apprentices were their own fathers[19]. In Southampton, the proportion was as high as 27% between 1670 and 1683[20]. Sometimes the motivation was financial; in London, it was not unknown for fathers to accept a premium from a charitable trust to apprentice their sons to themselves[21].

Apprenticeship usually involved parents or other sponsors entering into an indenture with a master[22]. Indentures were required by the 1563 statute. They set out the respective duties of master and apprentice, specified the term of service (often seven years, although longer for parish apprentices), and recorded the sum of money (the premium) paid to the master for the apprenticeship. In the medieval period there was probably no premium. By the beginning of the eighteenth century, when stamp duty was imposed on them, they were common (although not universal). The master might be required to supply the apprentice with clothing and tools. Sponsors might be required to provide for the apprentice if he became ill, or to pay compensation if the master suffered loss by the apprentice's mis-behaviour. The apprentice might receive some payment after he had gained experience. Some were to be paid a lump sum at the end of their term, and/or given a new suit of clothes. Apprentices were not generally permitted to trade on their own account, although sometimes this was allowed towards the end of their term.

Occasionally, masters were required to make provision for the general education of their charges, especially if they were young. This could include reading and writing, but these skills may have been learnt before indentures were signed. In London, the Goldsmiths Company accepted no apprentice 'without he can read and write'[23]. In Southampton, stipulations about education began to appear in the city's poor child register - but not in the general register - from the late seventeenth century[24]. Poor apprentices were generally younger.

Teaching in other subjects might also be required. A knowledge of accounts could be useful for tradesmen. Merchants and others might need to speak foreign languages, and their apprentices were sometimes sent to the continent to learn Dutch or French, Spanish or Portuguese. Francis Simpson was expected to spend the last years of his term in France or Spain[25]. A Great Yarmouth hosier's apprentice in 1627 was to spend half of each year in Holland[26]. Latin and Greek were required in some occupations, for example, surgery and compositing. The wardens of London's Scriveners Company had to examine apprentices, and could require masters to send them to a grammar school if their Latin was inadequate[27]. Religious education was normally assumed, although not necessarily specified in indentures. The *Book of common prayer* expected masters to ensure that their apprentices learnt the catechism, and an act of 1593 required masters to ensure that apprentices attended church.

Indentures for parish apprentices usually specified that the master was to ensure that the apprentice did not become a charge on his home parish during the term. Masters who were freemen were expected to help their apprentices gain their freedom at the end of their apprenticeship.

The choice of a master was determined by personal connections and recommendation. There were frequently family connections. Quaker families sought out Quaker masters for their children. Parents of other denominations also sought to find like-minded masters. In the eighteenth century, the development of newspapers made it possible for both masters and parents (and especially overseers) to advertise. Masters sought children from 'respectable families' who had the requisite 'honesty and sobriety'. They were likely to promise that the child would live as one of the family, and asked for a premium (although rarely specifying the amount, which was negotiable). In 1818, Hebbert & Salkelds, boot and shoemakers in the City, were advertising in the *Times* for 'a youth of good address, who has had a religious education; a moderate premium is expected'. Some apprentices went to live with their masters before formal indentures were signed. The relationship between master and apprentice depended upon a 'liking', and either party could back out before they were legally committed.

Factory owners also advertised widely for apprentices, promising humane treatment, asking for a 'moderate' premium, and expecting responses from parish overseers. If necessary, they would visit parishes - which could be many miles away - in order to negotiate terms.

Masters were not always suitable, or financially able to bear the cost of an apprentice. Occasionally, they, rather than the apprentice, absconded. In such cases, parish authorities were obliged to provide for the destitute apprentice and sought to prosecute the master. In other cases, both master and apprentice could find themselves in parish workhouses. If a master could no longer support an apprentice, or failed to comply with the terms of the indentures, they could be cancelled. The lack of an adequate diet, or adequate clothes, could attract the attention of the authorities. So could excessive harshness and violence on the master's part - although a degree of harshness was expected. Physical violence was generally thought to be necessary in order for an apprentice to learn his trade. Parish apprentices suffered particularly severely[28].

Apprentices sometimes had to serve several different masters in the course of their apprenticeship. A master who could no longer use the services of an apprentice could sell the remainder of the term to another master. This right was, however, open to abuse and was consequently strictly regulated by guilds[29]. If a master died, became insolvent or violated the indentures, Justices of the Peace could be asked to 'turn over' the apprentice to another master. In 1656, Thomas Grainger of Gloucester was turned over to Thomas Bailey, pinmaker. The register implies that he had originally been apprenticed to Henry Phenix, who had died. He had continued to serve Phenix's widow, Margaret, until she too died[30]. Note that records of turnovers may identify the widows of masters.

Masters could also simply disappear. In 1693, Francis Hutchings of Gloucester we turned over to a new master for the remainder of his term, his previous master, Benjamin Robbins, 'being gone off'[31].

There could also be positive reasons for changing masters. Craftsmen were sometimes skilled in different aspects of the same trade and apprentices might want to change masters in order to learn different skills. In London, an apprentice who wanted to join a livery company other than the Company for his own trade might seek a new master for that purpose.

Changes of masters may be recorded in apprenticeship registers. In 1777, the Company of Shipwrights of Newcastle upon Tyne recorded that George Wray, who had suffered 'hardship and ill treatment' from his master, had made choice of Thomas Curry as his new master to complete his apprenticeship'[32]. Oxford's register records that 9.1% of apprentices were 'turned over' in the eighteenth century[33] However, in the Gloucester register, a surprising number of boys were indentured twice without reference to the cancellation of earlier indentures[34].

The cancellation of indentures did not necessarily mean that the apprentice took a new master. Thomas Cox was 'discharged from his master ... for that William Powell is not capable of keepin an apprentice to follow the trade and not living in the city'[35]. His indentures were cancelled, but there is no record that he took another master. In Oxford, as has been noted, many turnovers were recorded, but there were also a number of instances where indentures seem to have been cancelled altogether[36].

Not every apprentice completed his term. Many felt that they had learnt their trade after two or three years, and moved on. Some died. Others migrated. In sixteenth-century London, over 800 apprentices either died or abandoned their training each year[37]. In seventeenth-century London, the drop-out rate was probably 50%[38]. In 1814, a Parliamentary committee estimated that 70% of London parish apprentices failed to serve their terms[39]. Testimonials proving that apprentices completed their terms survive for only 45% of the apprentices bound out by London's Foundling Hospital[40].

In the provinces, a surprisingly high proportion of apprentices failed to take up their freedom. Some returned to their home. Others moved elsewhere. Between 1641 and 1700, only c.25% of names recorded in Gloucester's apprenticeship registers are also recorded in its freemen's registers[41]. Substantial numbers of apprentices failed to serve their full terms. The mayor of Bristol complained in 1662 that many of those being transported to the Plantations were runaway apprentices[42]. Family historians should try to determine whether their apprentice ancestors completed their servitude.

It is also clear that not everyone served an apprenticeship. Norwich's population expanded considerably in the late seventeenth century, but the number of indentures enrolled actually fell. In the same period, London was attracting 8000 migrants every year, but only c.4000 apprentices[43].

There was no set method for an apprentice to learn his trade. He generally began by undertaking menial duties such as sweeping the floor or making the tea, all the while watching his master as he went about his business. He would gradually undertake more responsible tasks, until his skills were equal to those of his master. Towards the end of an apprenticeship, the apprentice could be very useful to his master. Some married their masters' daughters and inherited their businesses. Other threatened their masters' businesses. An apprentice who was about to establish his own business could easily attract his master's customers.

The hours of an apprentice were generally long - twelve to fourteen hours per day. In some trades, of course, daylight was required if work was to be done. Medieval guilds sometimes regulated apprentices' hours, as they suspected the quality of work done in the hours of darkness. In slack periods, there might be free time, but breaks were generally restricted to Christmas, Easter and a number of other festivals. Sundays were for church attendance.

Premiums varied widely, from nothing to £1000 and more. In the medieval period, they were not normally necessary. Indeed, in 1555 the Merchant Adventurers of Newcastle upon Tyne imposed a fine of £10 on any master who took a premium[44] - a sure sign that masters were flouting tradition, and that change was coming. By the seventeenth century, premiums were common. The Stamp Duty Act of 1709 required the amount of the premium to be stated in indentures. The law was not always complied with. Oxford masters were only fully compliant with this demand after 1750[45].

Sometimes premiums were paid by instalment. The amount depended on the status of the trade and the master, fluctuations in trade and the status of parents or sponsors. Luxury trades might require a higher premium. London's merchant tailors frequently required fathers to enter a substantial bond (perhaps £100 or more) for their son's good behaviour as an apprentice. The apprentice's family was buying an entrance to prosperity, but the master could suffer serious loss by an apprentice's mistakes and misbehaviour. The effect of high premiums on apprentices themselves were decried by Daniel Defoe; he regarded them as the cause of their unruliness. Apprentices who had paid them could not be treated as servants or subjected to the proper correction that they needed[46].

By contrast, the premium paid by poor law authorities were determined by the difficulties they had in finding masters willing to take on a parish apprentice. Nevertheless, premiums rarely exceeded £10. In London, the normal amount was £2. Sometimes, masters were required to enter into a bond to meet the terms of the indenture.

The age at which apprentices were bound varied. The average age of London apprentices was about 17[47]. A seven year term meant that service would be completed at age 24 - the usual age at which freedom was granted. Pauper apprentices were younger. It was argued that apprentices should be bound 'early whilst they be young and tractable, before idleness and the effects of a bad education make them unfit for service'[48]. To some extent, the age of the apprentice depended on his trade. Hard physical labour, such as bricklaying or smithing, demanded strength and therefore older boys. Younger children were particularly valuable to chimney sweeps: they were small enough to climb chimneys where masters could not. Trades such as husbandry and housewifery also offered a range of repetitive and unskilled tasks which small children could manage. Overseers frequently bound pauper children as young as 6 or 7 to these trades. It was not until 1816 that they were banned from apprenticing children aged under nine.

There were also variations in age due to family circumstances. Bereavement may have been the catalyst for many bindings. When Richard Skey bound himself apprentice to William Bradshawe in Woodstock, his father was 'recently deceased'[49]. John Fry, aged 10, had just become an orphan when the poor law authorities in Southampton bound him to John Foreman[50]. Many entries in the Southampton and Oxford apprenticeship registers record the father as being 'late of ... deceased'. Between 1631 and 1638, the proportion in Southampton was one-third[51]. In Gloucester, about a quarter of seventeenth-century apprentices were bound after the deaths of their father. In 1653, the figure was as high as 56%[52].

The distance that children had to travel to take up apprenticeships also varied. Most towns, especially London, depended on migrants for their continued growth, and apprentices formed a substantial proportion of those migrants. In Great Yarmouth and Ipswich, for example, over 50% of apprentices were migrants[53].

A few children travelled long distances to take up apprenticeships. 22 Norwich apprentices between 1510 and 1625 came from Cumberland. One came from as far away as Cornwall[54]. Long distance migration slackened in the late seventeenth century. In Gloucester, the proportion of apprentices who had travelled long distances to find masters shrank from about 13% in the early 1600s to 5% in the 1690s[55]. In Oxford, only 4.7% of apprentices travelled more than 25 miles in the late eighteenth century[56]. Many London apprentices came from the North of England during the sixteenth century. In the seventeenth century, more came from the Midlands. Apprentices from south-eastern counties predominated in the eighteenth century[57]. During the industrial revolution, some pauper children were sent many miles to work in the textile factories of the North. But the majority of apprentices found masters locally, either in their own communities or within 25 miles of their homes.

The social origins of apprentices were diverse. Attention has already been drawn to pauper apprentices, who were generally bound to the least desirable trades. At the other end of the social spectrum were the sons of gentlemen and esquires. The idea that gentility and apprenticeship were incompatible sometimes had to give way to hard economic reality[58]. Nevertheless, gentry children tended to be bound to the most desirable trades. In Interregnum London (1651-60), over 38% of apprentices in the Grocers' Company were the sons of the gentry, whereas they only made up 6% of Cordwainer apprentices[59].

In the seventeenth and eighteenth centuries, the number of gentlemen apprentices were increasing. Some commentators thought that this created problems. In Philip Massinger's comedy, *The City Madam*[60],

'the masters never prosper'd
Since gentlemens sons grew prentices: when we look
To have our business done at home, they are
Abroad in the tennis court, or in Partridge Alley
In Lambeth Marsh, or a cheating ordinary'

Despite increasing gentrification, however, in the mid seventeenth century the majority of apprentices in London were the children of artisans and tradesmen. They accounted for over 63% of butchers, and 50% of stationers[61].

Traditional apprenticeship gradually died out in most trades in the nineteenth century. The monopoly exercised by the guilds had been under attack for over a century, both from lawyers who argued that everyone had a natural right to trade, and from the proponents of free trade[62]. Legal decisions made the Statute of Artificers redundant. A Select Committee of the House of Commons reported in 1806 that, in the woollen industry, 'the system of apprenticeship had been in many parts of the country greatly disused'[63]. Growing awareness of the poor conditions which some parish apprentices faced led to legislation which imposed demands on masters: the Health and Morals of Apprenticeship Act of 1802 is one example. The legal requirement for tradesmen to undergo an apprenticeship disappeared with the abolition of the Statute of Artificers in 1814. Even the Poor Law Commissioners were not enthusiastic about it. Nevertheless, some apprentices continued to be bound. A number of Poor Law Unions were still binding a few boys in 1900, and Barnardo's were still sending child emigrants to Canada as apprentices[64].

CHAPTER TWO
Guild Apprenticeship and Civic Control

In the medieval period, craftsmen's guilds and companies were formed in many towns to offer mutual support, and to govern their trade. Sometimes, especially in London, the livery companies were very wealthy and able to provide the Crown with substantial supplies of money, men and munitions. Guilds enforced standards in manufacturing and retail; they exercised monopolies of particular trades; they controlled recruitment to their trades; and they cared for the welfare of their members and families. Guilds acquired a wide range of supervisory responsibilities. They tried to make sure that masters and apprentices were fulfilling their mutual responsibilities; that apprentices were competent before entering the freedom; and that the wider interests of the Guild were upheld. Their by-laws governed such matters as who could be a master; the number of apprentices masters could have; the conduct of apprentices; and the way in which indentures were enrolled and freedom granted. In some London companies, for example, indentures had not only to be enrolled, but the apprentice had to be examined in person by Company officers[65]. The Company of Saddlers of Newcastle upon Tyne laid down that masters had to be free for at least a year and a day before they took on an apprentice and that apprentices had to be aged at least 14 before they could enter indentures[66]. The same city's Company of Shipwrights levied fines on

13

shipwrights who took on too many apprentices[67]. The result of too many apprentices could be poor training, shoddy workmanship and too many journeymen for the work available[68].

Most apprentices were male. It has been estimated that only 2% of apprentices in sixteenth century London were female[69]. In early eighteenth century London, the variety of women's trades was considerable, but most were found in the food, drink, and entertainment trades, or in textiles and clothing. Not all companies were prepared to admit women, but some did. In 1665 James Windus and his wife Anne apprenticed Elizabeth Billingsley as a scrivener. The following year they took on Lucy Sanderson. When his wife died, James remarried, and in 1677 took on Margaret Alsop. He evidently preferred female apprentices[70].

The 'custom of London' was followed by many towns and cities. In Norwich, for example, rules laid down that every master had to be a freeman of the city, and a member of his craft guild. Apprenticeship had to be for a minimum term of seven years. The apprentice had to be freeborn, and not a villein, and the indenture had to be enrolled within twelve months and a day of being signed.

These rules were not necessarily enforced. In 1512, the Norwich Assembly had to insist on the need for registration. It ordered that 'in future all indentures of all and singular apprentices of any crafts taken within the city shall be enrolled and established before the Mayor of the said city within one quarter of a year next and immediately after their sealing. And if it shall happen that any such indenture shall be made and not enrolled in the said form the agreements of that apprentice shall be void and annulled, and indenture made thereon shall be of no strength'[71]. Similarly, by-laws made in Lancaster during the reign of Edward III, and confirmed under Queen Elizabeth, state 'that every ffreeman that takes any apprentice shall enroll his indentures in the courte book within a yeare and a day after he take the same apprentice upon paine to fforfeit for every default xxs. Also every ffreeman to pay for an enrolment xxs'[72]. In Gloucester, the Common Council decreed in 1613 that a register of apprentices was to be kept, 'wherein the true dates and terms of all indentures of apprentices shall be entered and registered'[73]. One wonders whether it had been the practice to falsify them?

A century after the Norwich Assembly's order, there were still problems. In 1622, the guilds themselves were instructed to enrol indentures, so that their registers could be compared with the enrolments made by the town clerk. Even so, many indentures were not enrolled[74]. Similar problems could be found in most cities.

There was usually a fee for enrolment, which some masters and apprentices may have tried to avoid[75]. Guild accounts may sometimes record these fees.

The records of Newcastle's Company of Hostmen[76] are full of orders and minutes relating to apprentices. The Guild's Court could prevent indentures being enrolled for a variety of reasons. Enrolment was refused to William Heath because he was a married man[77]. Joseph Watson's indentures stated that he was to train as a merchant, and he therefore could not be enrolled as a hostman[78]. In 1665, Henry Marlay was fined for using 'bad language' when his indentures were rejected[79]. The Court sought to prevent apprentices from trading on their own account[80], objected when an apprentice went to school for nine months without serving his master[81] and cancelled the indentures of apprentices who were absent from their master's service[82]. Similar episodes can be found in the records of the City's merchant adventurers[83] and in many other guild records.

A final assessment of an apprentice's training was frequently made before he was admitted to the freedom of his guild. Guild officers had to be satisfied with the quality of an apprentice's workmanship before he could be admitted. Bristol's Company of Soapmakers demanded 'further triall of his workmanship of chaundlynge' before they would permit John Slye to trade as a chandler in 1571[84]. Some guilds required the submission of examples of workmanship. London needlemakers, for example, demanded a sample of 50 needles of various sizes[85].

At the end of an apprenticeship, apprentices in boroughs were frequently eligible to become freemen. Custom did, however, vary from place to place. It was also possible to become a freeman by inheritance, by property ownership, by matrimony or by purchase. There were perhaps 100 boroughs where apprentices had the right to become freemen. The rights and privileges of freemen varied from place to place. Generally, however, freemen enjoyed a monopoly of certain trades, and might be exempted from various taxes and customs duties. They also sometimes formed the electorate for the election of Members of Parliament and city officers - and may be listed in poll books. Trading rights were important before 1700, but their importance was diminishing. In London, the freedom gradually became a mark of social prestige, rather than a recognition of a master's right to trade[86]. In the eighteenth and nineteenth centuries, members of the livery companies gradually ceased to practise the trades which companies represented. Between 1765 and 1801, only 68% of apprentices bound to the city's Cordwainers actually learnt the trade. 11% were bound in order to learn the trades of other London livery companies; 21% were bound to other trades[87]. In Gloucester, the common council protested in 1680 that burgesses were taking apprentices 'not to teach them their trade, but to let them in to the freedom of this city'[88]. The proportion of freemen who had served an apprenticeship was declining in the late seventeenth and eighteenth centuries, whilst the proportion who had purchased their freedom was rising[89]. This reflected the fact that the status was becoming less important for tradesmen, but more important for politics. In 1729, Parliament enacted that no freeman could vote until 12 months after his admission.

The demand for free trade gradually reduced the trading rights of freemen, and the Municipal Reform Act 1835 abolished them. Possession of the freedom gradually came to be seen as imposing a heavy burden of civic responsibilities. That was why a number of leading Norwich freemen requested to be disenfranchised in the early eighteenth century[90]. The freedom remained important in many boroughs only because it gave freemen the right to vote in borough and Parliamentary elections. That right was removed by the Reform Act of 1832. The status of freeman became merely honorific after the two acts of 1832 and 1835. It ceased to have any practical importance. London was an exception to this rule. Its freemen continued to vote in municipal elections until 1867; liverymen of city companies retained that right until 1918 and were separately listed in electoral registers until 1948[91].

Apprenticeship was not the only route to becoming a freeman, although eligibility did vary from place to place. In Newcastle upon Tyne, only those who were apprenticed to freemen were eligible, except when the Corporation wanted to bestow an honorary freedom[92]. In many corporations, however, the freedom could be acquired by patrimony, or by redemption, i.e. purchase. The sons of freemen were generally eligible for election to the freedom of their city, regardless of whether they had served an apprenticeship. And men who had sufficient wealth could purchase their way in. It could be a profitable investment, or, later, a means of political influence. The Statute of Artificers had laid down that trades could only be followed if the tradesman had served an apprenticeship. This rule was frequently breached by those who claimed freedom by patrimony, but had not served a master for seven years[93].

Some apprentices became freemen immediately on completing their term. Others worked for a few years before applying for admission. In Bristol, between 1600 and 1630, over 44% waited for more than 2 years[94]. In London, an ordinance of the Common Council made in 1556 laid down that men could only be admitted when they had attained the age of 24. It was thought an earlier age encouraged 'over hastie marriages', which could lead to poverty[95]. Occasionally, admission was made on condition of accepting a parish apprentice. John Enough, shoemaker of Southampton, had to accept a child aged 4 as an apprentice for 17 years(!) in order to become a freeman of his guild[96].

Not all apprentices actually took up their freedom. It has already been pointed out that a substantial number failed to complete their term of servitude. For those who did, it was common practice to continue to serve the same master as a waged journeyman for some years. In Southampton, indentures sometimes required an apprentice to serve his master as a hired servant for a year at the end of his apprenticeship[97]. The money that could be earned as a journeyman might be essential in order to establish a business.

There was sometimes a considerable lapse of time between completing an apprentice's term of service, and taking up the freedom. In Sheffield, a period as long as 45 years has been noted[98]. There was usually a fee for admission. In Queen Anne's Lancaster, the sons of freemen had to pay £1, apprentices £1.6s.8d.[99]

Applicants for the freedom did not always obtain it. They had to prove that they had served their full term, and that their work was up to scratch. Thomas Taylor's petition to be admitted to Newcastle's Company of Hostmen was rejected, because 'he did not make due service to his master, but served Henry Waters, an unfreeman, and forreigne to this Company ... and served foreigners after'[100]. In Oxford, the register of apprentices notes that John Coldery was not to be allowed his freedom, 'the binding appearing to be clandestine'[101].

CHAPTER THREE

Parish Apprentices

P overty and unemployment were endemic during the industrial revolution and earlier. The poor were fortunate, however, that the church regarded the relief of poverty as a duty falling on all Christians, and that the state took on the responsibility of ensuring that poverty was relieved. That responsibility was delegated to parish overseers of the poor at the end of the sixteenth century. One of their most serious problems was what to do with pauper children, especially bastards and the infirm.

The extent of the problem can be judged from the records of Rackenford, Devon[102]. A comparison of apprenticeship registers and indentures with the baptism register shows that the proportion of bindings to christenings varied from 3% in 1770-79 to as high as 24% in 1800-1809. Certain families recur repeatedly in parish apprenticeship registers: no less than 20 members of the Flew family were parish apprentices in Rackenford between 1728 and 1844.

In Devon, Marshall[103] tells us, the response of the authorities was 'to put out the children of paupers, boys more particularly, at the age of seven or eight years, to farmers and others; and to bind them as apprentices until

they be twenty-one years of age'. He described this as 'an easy and ready way of disposing of the children of paupers, and is fortunate for the children thus disposed of, as ensuring them labor and industry, and providing them with better sustenance than they could expect to receive from their parents'. Sadly, however, they were not well treated, but subjected to 'a state of the utmost drudgery', with the consequence that 'they desert their servitude and fill the provincial presses with advertisements for runaway apprentices'. William Bailey agreed. In a treatise he wrote in 1758, he argued that 'Many of those who take parish apprentices are so inhuman, as to regard only the pecuniary considerations, and having once received that, they, by ill usage and undue severity, often drive the poor creatures from them.'[104].

Apprenticeship was a more efficient means of controlling the poor than the alternative of requiring them to enter service. Service normally lasted for a term of twelve months. Apprenticeship lasted at least seven years.

Pauper children, and especially bastards, were viewed by the authorities in a variety of ways. Firstly, they were a costly drain on the poor rates. Apprenticeship relieved the parish of the need to maintain these children. It provided a means of keeping down the poor rate. If a child could be apprenticed outside of the parish, it would lose its right of settlement in that parish, and thus end any further liability to the parish. Secondly, pauper children were thought to be a potential threat to society. The indiscipline of youth, and the threatened hordes of beggars, could be controlled to some extent by apprenticing them. Apprenticeship was a useful means of social control. Thirdly, they were an excellent source of cheap and easily disciplined labour. Factory owners during the early industrial revolution frequently recruited their labour force by apprenticing pauper children. Fourthly, and lastly, they were objects of compassion and charity. Charity, however, meant that they should be enabled to earn their own living at the earliest possible moment. Work provided a route out of poverty.

Parish authorities were keen to reduce their liabilities, but could be tardy in performing their duties towards parish apprentices. Once a child was apprenticed, which could be as early as age 7, many parish officers considered themselves to be relieved of their responsibilities, and took little trouble to supervise masters. The records reveal few attempts to assess potential masters' suitability to undertake their duties. Once a child had been bound apprentice, supervision of his progress by parish officers was spasmodic, although it was rare for the welfare of parish apprentices to be totally neglected by their guardians. Children apprenticed in the textile factories of the North were occasionally visited by officers from their home parish. Some concern for their welfare was shown - but that concern was rarely translated into action[105].

The criteria which parents used to determine their children's future trades were quite different from the criteria used by poor law authorities. The ideal was set by Bristol's Corporation of the Poor, who argued that the master should 'be a man of ability and honesty also of some sort of employment or faculty lest otherwise the child be ill treated and thereby tempted to forsake his service or else consume his time idly without learning any thing whereby he may live hereafter'[106]. In practice, such considerations were frequently ignored.

Overseers were primarily concerned with their own short-term interests, not with the long-term employability of the child. According to Sir John Fielding, writing in 1786, 'the chief view of the overseer is to get rid of the object and fix his settlement in another parish'[107]. It was a common practice, when a master lived in another parish, to withhold the payment of the premium until the apprentice had gained a settlement in that parish. The overseers could thus ensure that any future liability to support the apprentice from the poor rates would fall on the master's parish, not their own[108]. Premiums were kept as low as possible, thus restricting the range of trades available to pauper children. In some parishes, pauper children were allotted to ratepayers by rota or ballot. In rural areas, substantial farmers could easily find work for idle hands. From 1696, those who refused to accept pauper apprentices could be fined. Such fines could be an important source of parochial finance, but they could also be the cause of much friction in parish life[109]. The power of binding was frequently capriciously exercised, and the subject of much complaint. Samuel Wilberforce objected when in 1843 he was asked to pay a £10 fine for failing to take an apprentice seven years earlier[110]. A degree of compulsion was sometimes needed to persuade masters to take on poor children. The premium that was offered was frequently only sufficient to attract masters who were indigent themselves. They sometimes took on the responsibility purely for the premium, not because they had any work for them. In the words of the Poor Law Commissioners, 'the premiums offered with the children proved an irresistible temptation to needy persons to apply for an apprentice'[111]. Such masters frequently defaulted on their obligations, encouraging their apprentices to abscond or claiming poor relief themselves.

As for the parents, although they might be consulted, they had no legal rights in the process of binding, and they were frequently not mentioned in the indentures of parish apprentices. They could object to the binding of their children, but, if they did so, they were likely to suffer financially. In 1796, Bristol parents were threatened with the suspension of their relief payments if they objected to the placement of their children[112].

Reluctance to accept a pauper child as an apprentice was partly based on the stigma attached to pauperism. It could also be based on the poor health of particular children. Parishes were keen to bind illegitimate children, the disabled, and the sick. They were particularly liable to be long-term drains on the rates - but were also those who were least attractive to potential masters. Where possible, overseers stressed the physical strength and good health of their children when advertising for masters.

Paupers were frequently apprenticed to occupations which had little or no long term future. They were regarded as providing a cheap supply of labour, and the authorities sometimes paid scant regard either to their interests, or to the interests of others in the trade. The availability of parish apprentices depressed the wages of many journeymen. Overseers took no account of the fact that too many children were being apprenticed to certain trades[113]. Children were frequently apprenticed to labour intensive occupations which required little skill and in which even the youngest children could be useful. In 1608, the Privy Council ordered Quarter Sessions to ensure that poor children were bound, 'specially to husbandrie and huswiferie'[114]. Even a seven year old could pick stones from a field or scare the crows.

The easy availability of labour from pauper children presented an opportunity for early industrialists, who needed a constant supply of labour. James Harris of Coventry recruited no fewer than 73 boys as weaving apprentices from Warwickshire and Northamptonshire in the late eighteenth century[115]. Some travelled much further. Almost 500 parish apprentices from London can be traced in the employment of William Cuckney & Co of Cuckney, Nottinghamshire, between 1786 and 1805[116]. Parish apprentices were unencumbered with parents, there were many available, absconding was difficult, and they were cheap. They were therefore an attractive source of labour for textile factories, so much so that professional agents were used by many companies to recruit them[117]. Abuse of the institution was easy, and sometimes poor law officers recognised the fact. The Bristol Corporation of the Poor was cautious in 1795 when an application for children was made from Preston, and suspended a similar application from Loughborough in 1796[118]. The magistrate who investigated conditions at Emscote Mill on behalf of a Select Committee in 1816 declared that he would never 'sign an indenture to a cotton mill so long as (he) lived'[119]. Nevertheless, it has recently been argued that apprentices in textile factories 'often acquired a training which provided a basis for adult employment'[120]. Honeyman has identified 3,332 paupers from London who worked in northern textile factories between 1786 and 1816[121]. They frequently stayed with their masters on completing their terms. Businesses that looked after their apprentices were more likely to succeed in the longer term[122]. And former apprentices who had served their terms in factories were preferred by employers[123].

Young children were needed in some trades, such as chimney sweeping, where smallness was essential. Girls were frequently apprenticed to housewifery, or to the clothing trades, neither of which offered long-term security. Certain trades became increasingly pauperised. There was only a limited range of occupations open to paupers; they were frequently hazardous and injurious to health, and offered no prospects.

For girls, there was an even more serious problem: sexual abuse. Some overseers tried to ensure that girls were only bound to women. But most pauper apprentices were placed with whoever could be persuaded to take them, and their masters were rarely supervised by the authorities. Most apprentices had limited contact with their parents. Pauper apprentices frequently had none. The consequences could be disastrous for girls.

The differences between pauper apprentices and apprentices sponsored by their relatives can be clearly seen by comparing the entries in Southampton's 'general register' of apprentices and its 'poor child register'. In 1609-10, when both registers began, the masters to whom the first five apprentices were bound in the 'general register' included a grocer, a woollen draper, a tailor, a woolcomber, and a mercer. In the 'poor child register' the first five masters included a joiner, a serge weaver, a blacksmith, a glover, and one unstated. A mercer was of much higher status than a glover. A similar distinction can be seen in the Kidderminster carpet industry. Those who learnt the craft of carpet weaving were apprenticed by their parents or by charities. The few pauper apprentices in the industry were employed as drawers, who set up the frames on which carpets were woven. This was an occupation for young people with nimble fingers, but it did not require great skill. There was no future in it[124].

The Poor Law Amendment Act of 1834 signaled a change in official attitudes towards parish apprentices. The new Poor Law Commissioners were not enthusiastic about the idea of apprenticing the children of paupers. It did not seem to comply with the principle of 'less eligibility', whereby those who received relief were expected to be less well-off than those who did not. Under the new regime, masters could no longer be compelled to accept apprentices. And paupers aged 14 or over could no longer be compelled to be bound. Many unions began to provide education and industrial training in their workhouses. Nevertheless, guardians continued to apprentice some of the young people in their charge. At the end of the century, many were still being sent to Grimsby to serve apprenticeship on Grimsby trawlers. By then, the practice was attracting increasing criticism. The *London Figaro* reported in 1873 that Grimsby had 'a system of slavery as infamous as any system of slavery ever devised'[125]. Its criticism was aimed at the treatment of fishing apprentices who had committed some misdemeanor. In practice, boys could, and did, have their indentures annulled. Between 1880 and 1909, 5,176 sets of indentures were signed, of which 814 were annulled[126]. Many others simply absconded.

CHAPTER FOUR
Charity Apprentices

T he child who gained the support of a charity endowed to support apprentices was much more fortunate than the parish apprentice. Many of these charities were established between the sixteenth and the nineteenth centuries. The reports of the Charity Commission provide much information about them. A number are mentioned in the published registers of Coventry[127], Oxford[128], Southampton[129] and Gloucester[130]. The Colyton Feoffees were a general charity who occasionally gave money for binding apprentices[131]. A number of county charities, frequently named 'Feasts', were established in the eighteenth and nineteenth centuries to fund apprenticeships[132]. The apprenticeship register of the Wiltshire Society, which was established by the county gentry in London in 1817, has been published[133]. London's Foundling Hospital, set up to look after abandoned children, funded apprenticeships for its charges[134]. Westminster's French Protestant Charity School apprenticed many of its former pupils[135].

Charities offered a range of benefits. Some offered both schooling and apprenticeship; some paid premiums for indentures; some purchased tools to help apprentices establish their own businesses when they finished their

term. A Wakefield charity was reported to give apprentices £20 to establish themselves in trade on the completion of their terms[136].

The children who benefited tended to be the orphans of tradesmen and craftsmen who had been respected in their communities, although some charities extended eligibility to the poor in general. The children of paupers who had received poor relief, however, were frequently excluded. A few charities required their apprentices to attend the Church of England regularly; others expected a certain level of education from their beneficiaries.

Local authorities were frequently made responsible for administration. In corporate towns, where most charities were based, this was required by an act of 1610. Alderman Holliday, for example, bequeathed £500 to the City of Gloucester in 1624, in order to apprentice 'four boys who have had an honest education ... and whose parents do want means thereunto'[137]. The fund was administered by the Council, and names of apprentices are sometimes recorded in its minutes. Some names are also recorded in the city's apprentice registers. A few beneficiaries were pauper children. Most charities offered support to children from a particular place, frequently the birthplace of the founder. Many were founded by tradesmen and craftsmen who had prospered, and wanted others to share their prosperity. Eligibility was set out in the foundation deeds, which were frequently the founders' wills.

Guilds also ran charities. Exeter's Crispin's Charity[138] was administered by the city's Incorporation of Weavers, Fullers and Shearmen, and took the form of an annuity of £10, to be shared between two apprentices. The money was used to provide apprenticeship premiums, and to help them set up in trade. Many indentures survive; so do various lists, accounts, and other papers[139].

1. Tuckers Hall, Exeter, home of Exeter's Incorporation of Weavers, Tuckers & Shearmen. Decisions about Crispin's Charity, which supported apprentices, were made here.

Some charities had no connection with either city or guild authorities. The Wiltshire Society[140] was founded by prominent Wiltshiremen in London in 1817, and aimed 'to apprentice the children of the deserving poor belonging to the County of Wiltshire, residing in London, who might otherwise be destitute of the means of acquiring a comfortable subsistence throughout life'. From 1859, it also apprenticed children resident in Wiltshire. Funds were raised by annual subscription and by donation. It was run by its members. The number of apprentices elected each year depended on available funds. Its registers give the names of apprentices, their parents and their masters, together with the residence and the trade of the latter. They also record the premium paid, the term of the apprenticeship and the date of indentures. Annual reports are also available, which sometimes give additional information.

Direct charitable giving by individuals is also recorded. In Southampton, Mrs. Elizabeth Clungeon made a gift of 50s when John Palmer was bound apprentice to Robert Veverell in 1670[141]. Alderman Clutterbuck of Gloucester gave money to enrol two apprentices in 1660[142].

CHAPTER FIVE

Introduction

Avariety of sources for tracing apprentices are available. The basic document is the apprenticeship indenture. Registers of apprentices were kept by guild and city authorities, and by parish and union officers. Records of admittance as a freeman may record the date an apprenticeship ended, and the name of the master. Other city records may provide more information. In London, between 1694 and 1861, a tax for the relief of orphans was imposed on all bindings, and registers were kept. Between 1710 and 1804, the national government imposed stamp duty on apprenticeship indentures, and again registers were kept.

Apprenticeship is also recorded incidentally in a variety of other records. If indentures or enrolments are found amongst the records of boroughs and guilds, check to see whether their other archives contain any relevant information. Churchwardens' and overseers' accounts, settlement examinations, court records, Parliamentary papers, newspapers, and other sources can all yield useful information. These can be found in local and national record offices[143], in libraries, and on the internet[144]. Records are not necessarily in obvious places. For example, 34 indentures from Skelmersdale, Yorkshire, can be found in the British Library[145]. Numerous original sources can be traced by using the National Archives search page: **www.nationalarchives.gov.uk/search**. The databases available here cover

both the National Archives own holdings, and the collections of numerous local record offices. The latter are covered by A2A: Access to Archives, which can be searched here, but is also available separately at **www.nationalarchives.gov.uk/a2a**. In some cases, very detailed calendars of particular collections are provided, including names. However, it is important to appreciate that, extensive as they are, these databases do not list everything that is available. Many collections remain uncatalogued. Some record offices do not contribute to A2A, but maintain catalogues on their own websites.

Many sources have been published by local record societies and family history societies, amongst others. The 'further reading' listed below give details of apprenticeship records in print. However, this only covers works specifically devoted to apprenticeship. There are also many record publications of churchwardens' accounts, settlement examinations, wills, court records, and other sources, which cannot be listed here (although some are referred to in footnotes). Many can be identified by consulting the Bibliography of British and Irish History: **www.brepolis.net/publishers/pdf/Brepolis_BBIH_EN.pdf**. This may be available through University libraries. The publications of family history societies are usually listed on their websites[146]. Most published sources are held by the Society of Genealogists **www.sog.org.uk**. They can also be found in many other libraries.

There are problems in using these sources. Researchers need to be aware that, although printed editions of registers can be very useful, nevertheless, they are transcripts. Their accuracy depends on their editors. Some editors are well qualified for their task; others are not. Printed editions should always, if possible be compared with the original sources to check their accuracy. Indexes do not reflect the full content of the documents indexed; they are merely finding aids. The fact that there is no index entry for a particular name does not necessarily mean that the name cannot be found in the document indexed. It is quite possible that the indexer simply missed a particular entry. Be aware, too, that names could be spelt in many different ways. Do not assume that the spelling of a particular name has always been the same. Check alternative spellings if you cannot find the index entry you are looking for.

The use of Latin in early documents may also pose difficulties, as may early forms of handwriting[147]. These should not be regarded as insurmountable difficulties. The researcher should always remember that the document before him was meant to be read. Much of the information in indentures and registers in particular is common form, and constantly repeated. Even if the whole document cannot be read, it should not be too difficult to pick out names, dates and other important details.

It is also important to appreciate that original sources are not always correct. In particular, it is likely that early apprenticeship registers are not as complete a record as they should be.

CHAPTER SIX
Apprenticeship Indentures

A pprenticeship indentures provide more information about apprentices than most other types of record. Two copies of every indenture were made, one for the apprentice, the other for the master. They were written on a single sheet, and indented by cutting a wavy or jagged line between the two copies. If any dispute arose, their genuineness could be demonstrated by re-uniting the two copies.

Many indentures can be found amongst city archives. Guilds and civic authorities frequently required them to be deposited, as well as being enrolled. In London, for example, the indentures of those who became freemen of the City were kept from 1681. They are filed in the City's freedom admission papers in the London Metropolitan Archives. In Devon, many indentures survive in the Exeter City Archives (now in Devon Record Office) from the seventeenth century. Some are originals, others have been abstracted. Many were written on printed forms, which were first introduced in the seventeenth century[148].

Apprenticeship indentures for parish apprentices frequently survive amongst parochial archives, and can be found in local record offices. Many parishes bound children to seamen; after 1824, their indentures were filed with the records of the Registrar General of Shipping and Seamen. Only a selection of the original indentures survive; these can be found in the National Archives, class BT 151 for 1854-1950. An index to all of these indentures, 1824-1953, is in BT 150. Indentures for fishing apprentices required by an act of 1894 are in the National Archives, class BT 152 for 1895-1935.

Private indentures which were not enrolled did not attract the attention of the authorities, and rarely survive. Some examples of private indentures can be found amongst the 1500 indentures held by the Society of Genealogists in its Crisp and Clench collection or original indentures[149]. Others can occasionally be found amongst estate and family papers in record offices.

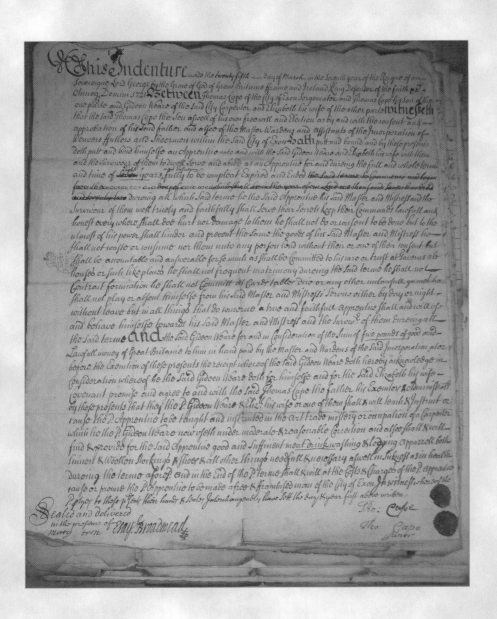

2. Apprenticeship Indenture for Thomas Cape, 1721, which is transcribed on p.34-35

Example 1

The following transcript of an apprenticeship indenture is from the Exeter City Archives, now held by Devon Record Office[150]. Note that the premium was paid by Exeter's Incorporation of Weavers, Fullers and Shearmen, although the trade the apprentice was to enter was that of a carpenter. Note too that, at the end of the apprenticeship, the master was expected to ensure that his apprentice became a freeman of the City of Exeter. He does not appear to have done so, since his name does not appear in the freemen's register[151]. The indenture identifies the father and the son; it also gives the names of his master and his mistress:

'This indenture made the twentyfifth day of March in the seventh year of the reigne of our sovereigne lord George by the Grace of God of Great Britaine France and Ireland King Defender of the Faith &c Annoq Dominie 1721 BETWEEN Thomas Cape of the City of Exon sergemaker and Thomas Cape his son of the one parte and Gideon Weare of the said city carpenter and Elizabeth his wife of the other parte WITNESSETH that the said Thomas Cape the son as well of his own free will and election as by and with the consent and approbation of his said father and alsoe of the Master Wardens and Assistants of the Incorporation of Weavers Fullers and Sheermen within the said city of Exon HATH putt and bound and by these presents doth putt and bind himselfe an apprentice unto and with the said Gideon Weare and Elizabeth his wife with them and the survivour of them to dwell serve and abide as an apprentice for and dureing the full and whole terme and time of ~~seven~~ eight[152] years next ensueing[153] fully to be compleat expired and ended ~~the said terme to commence and begin from the ... day of ... which shall be in the yere of our Lord one thousand seven hundred and twenty two~~[154] dureing all which said terme the said apprentice his said master and mistress and the survivour of them well truely and faithfully shall serve their secrets keep their commands lawful and honest everywhere shall doe hurt nor damage to them he shall not do or consent to be done but to the utmost of his power shall hinder and prevent the same the goods of his said Master and Mistress he shall not waste or consume nor them unto any person lend without their or one of their consent but shall be accountable and answerable for so much as shall be committed to his care or trust at taverns ale houses or such like places he shall not frequent matrimony dureing the said terme he shall not contract fornication he shall not committ at cards tables dice or any other unlawfull games he shall not play or absent himself from his said Master and Mistress's service either by day or night without leave but in all things that do concerne a true and faithfull apprentice shall and will use and behave himselfe towards his said Master and Mistress and the surviv^r of them dureing all the said terme AND the said Gideon Weare for and in consideration of the sum of five pounds of good and lawfull money of Great Britaine to him in hand paid by the Master and Wardens of the said Incorporation at or before the execution of these presents the receipt whereof the said Gideon Weare doth hereby acknowledge in consideration whereof he the s^d Gideon Weare doth for himselfe and for the said Elizabeth his wife Covenant promise and agree to and with the said Thomas Cape the father his executors and administrators by these presents that they the s^d Gideon Weare & Eliz^th his wife or one of them shall & will teach & instruct or cause the s^d apprentice to be taught and instructed in the art trade mistery or occupation of a carpenter which he the s^d Gideon Weare now useth under moderate & reasonable correction and alsoe shall & will find & provide for the said apprentice good and sufficient meat drink washing & lodging apparrell both linnen & woollen stockings & shoes & all other things needfull & necessary as well in sickness as in health dureing the terme afores^d and in the end of the s^d terme shall & will at the costs & charges of the s^d apprentice cause or procure the s^d apprentice to be made a free & franchised man of the City of Exon. In witness whereof the s^d ptyes to these presents their hands & seales interchangeably have sett the day & year first above written

Tho Cape
Tho Cape Juner

Sealed and delivered in the presence of:
Mary Tren
Esay Broadmead'

Example 2.

The following transcript offers an example of an indenture that was entered into Exeter's apprenticeship 'book of enrolments'[155]. The book contained abstracts, not full transcripts, and it may be doubted whether the work of the scribe was entirely accurate: it is probable that the responsibility for meat and drink for the first six months of the term actually fell to the grandfather. If that was not the case, why would this period be singled out? There are three other features that are worth noting. The apprentice is being bound by his grandfather, and was probably an orphan. His proposed trade is the same as his grandfather's, that of cabinet maker. The parishes of both parties are stated; this may help with identifying entries in parish registers:

'Inrolled 22nd November 1819. Skardon. James, grandson of John Nicholls of Allhallows on the Walls, cabinet maker, by indenture dated 22nd November 1819 binds himself an apprentice to William Nicholls Skardon of St. Edmonds, cabinet maker, for the term of seven years from the said date. The master covenants with the grandfather to find the apprentice cloathes and wearing apparel of all sorts and the making and mending the same and physick and attendance in sickness during the said term and also meat and drink during the first half year, and that the apprentice shall faithfully serve the master during the term. The master covenants with the grandfather to teach the apprentice the trade of a cabinet maker and to find him meat and drink during the last 6 years and half and also lodging and washing during the whole of the said term.

One part only on a 20^s stamp and executed by all the parties in the presence of Geo Stabback Junr'

Example 3.

This example is from the same book as the previous one, and, again, this is an abstract from the original indentures, not the indentures themselves. In this case the apprentice is bound by his mother, who was presumably a widow, to the trade of jeweller and goldsmith. This was a high status trade, and the premium of £20 recognises this. Unusually, the apprentice was to live with his mother. Unfortunately, no parish is named:

> 'Hall. Clement, son of Elizabeth Hall of the City of Exeter, by indenture dated 9th August 1825, binds himself as apprentice to John Sweet and John Henry Sweet of the same city, jewellers and goldsmiths, for the term of seven years from the date. The masters, in consideration of a premium of £20 covenant to teach the apprentice the trade of a jeweller and goldsmith, and to pay him 5/- a week during the last four years of the term. The mother covenants to find the apprentice meat drink washing lodging apparel physic and attendance.
>
> One part only engrossed and one pound stamp and executed by all parties in the presence of Fra[s] Drake Clerk to Mr. Zech[r] Turner'

Example 4.

This indenture was made by overseers of the poor on a form 'printed by J. Hayes, Dartmouth Street, Westminster, for His Majesty's Stationery Office'[156]. The words in brackets were inserted by hand. The form left no space for the name of the apprentice's father, who had no legal status in the binding. It does, however, give his age. That, combined with the fact that he was the responsibility of the overseers of Heavitree, indicates where his baptism should be searched for. Note that, even in the suburban parish of Heavitree, at this date apprentices could still be bound to husbandry:

> 'This Indenture made the [eighteenth] day of [July] in the [forty third] year of the reign of our Sovereign Lord [George the third], by the Grace of God, of the United Kingdom of Great Britain and Ireland King, Defender of the Faith, and so forth, and in the year of our Lord 18[03] WITNESSETH That [John Wolland and William Prew] Church-Wardens of the [parish of Heavitree in the County of Devon] And [the said John Wolland and Robert Snow] Overseers of the Poor of the said [parish] by and with the consent of his Majesty's Justices of the Peace for the said [county] whose names are hereunto subscribed, have put and placed and by these presents do put and place [Mathew Brinfield] aged [10 years] or thereabouts, a poor child of the said [parish] apprentice to [Thomas Salter for Windout Hill] with him to dwell and serve from the day

of the date of these presents, until the said apprentice shall accomplish [his] full age of [twenty one years] according to the statute in that case made and provided; during all which term the said apprentice h[is] said [master] faithfully shall serve in all lawful businesses, according to h[is] power, wit, and ability; and honestly, orderly, and obediently in all things demean and behave h[im] self towards h[is] said M[aster] and all h[is] during the said term. AND the said [Thomas Salter] for h[im]self, h[is] executors and administrators, doth covenant and grant to and with the said Church-Wardens and Overseers, and every of them, their, and every of their executors and administrators, and their and every of their successors, for the time being, by these presents, that he the said [Thomas Salter] the said apprentice in [husbandry work] shall and will teach and instruct, or cause to be taught and instructed, in the best way and manner that he can [during the said term] the term aforesaid, find provide and allow unto the said Apprentice meet, competent and sufficient meat drink apparel, lodging washing, and other things necessary and fit for an apprentice PROVIDED ALWAYS that the said last mentioned covenant on the said [Master] his executors and administrators to be done and performed shall continue and be in force for no longer time than three calendar months next after the death of the said [Master] in case the said [Master] shall happen to die during the continuance of such apprenticeship according to the provisions of an act passed in the thirty-second year of the reign of King George the Third, intituled 'An Act for the further Regulation of Parish Apprentices') AND also shall and will so provide for the said Apprentice, that [he] be not any way a charge to the said [parish] or parishioners of the same: but of and from all charge shall and will save the said [parish] harmless and indemnified during the said Term.

In witness whereof, the parties abovesaid to these present indentures interchangeably have set their hands and seals the day and year first above written.

Thos Salter

Sealed and Delivered in the Presence of
Thos Channon

> We whose Names are here under-written Justices of the Peace for the [County] aforesaid (whereof one is of the Quorum) Do consent to the putting forth [Mathew Brinfield] an apprentice according to the Intent and Meaning of this Indenture
>
> R^t Lydstone Newcombe
> John Baring'

CHAPTER SEVEN
Borough Apprenticeship Records[157]

M any boroughs kept records of apprentices bound to freemen. They could expect to become freemen themselves in due course. In 1613, the Common Council of Gloucester decreed that:

> 'henceforth no apprentice shall be bound to serve any man within this city but before the mayor of this city and in his presence, and that for that purpose a book or register shall be kept in the custody of the said mayor ... wherein the true dates and terms of all indentures or apprentices shall be entered and registered.'[158].

Registers usually name the apprentice, his father, and their place of residence. The father's occupation is usually given. The master, his occupation, and his residence are also recorded, together with the term of servitude, the premium paid, and the date of the indenture. Sometimes registers are more detailed, recording, for example, that the master had to provide apparel for the apprentice at the end of his indentures, that the apprentice changed masters, or that wages were to be paid. In some cases,

detailed abstracts of indentures were kept. In other cases, the indentures themselves were deposited in city or guild archives. If indentures are available, it may be possible to compare them with registers[159]. Apprentices may also be mentioned in other borough records. Court records are discussed below. Accounts frequently record payments made for enrolment of indentures, and for admission to the freedom. In Woodstock, Laurence Williow and Leonard Witham both paid 20d for admission to the freedom in 1640/41[160]. Such entries can be checked against apprenticeship registers, and may sometimes give additional information.

Registers of apprentices do not necessarily include every entry that should have been made. Under-registration was a serious problem for the authorities, as may be seen by the many references to it in the minutes of their proceedings. For example, it is likely that many apprentices who benefited from the Southampton charity set up under Mrs. Knowles' legacy in 1634 were not entered in the apprentices' register[161]. Her aim had been to pay for the binding of two apprentices every year. Only 5 entries in the registers were made in the following century. Either her funds were mis-applied or the register is incomplete.

It is also likely that many pauper apprentices were not registered, or, at least, that separate registers were kept. They were not expected to become free[162]. This is not always the case; many paupers were entered in the Coventry registers[163].

CHAPTER EIGHT

Freemen s Registers

Apprentices in boroughs were usually eligible for election to the freedom on completion of their apprenticeships. Borough charters frequently restricted the right to trade within borough boundaries to freemen, and consequently possession of the freedom was a valuable economic right. The authorities therefore needed to know who was eligible for admission to the freedom. That was why apprenticeship registers were kept. They also needed to know who had been admitted to the freedom. Hence the need for freemen's registers. These record details of admittance to the freedom and may give the names of parents and masters. They are also likely to note the reasons for granting admission. The qualification required for admission varied between boroughs, but, broadly, the freedom could be purchased; it could be inherited; or it could be acquired by apprenticeship. Registers record all admissions, regardless of qualification. A number have been published, including those for Canterbury, Chester, Exeter, Guildford, Lancaster, London, Newcastle and Norwich[164]. Sometimes, as in Newcastle[165], admissions were entered in guild books or other court records that contain much other miscellaneous information. At Great Yarmouth, and no doubt elsewhere, payment for admission to the freedom are recorded on the borough court rolls from 1429.

Apprenticeship and freedom registers, used together, may make it possible to trace apprentices at both the beginning and end of their terms of servitude. It may also be possible to trace apprentices who became freemen and masters, and who took on their own apprentices. Sometimes, it is possible to use apprenticeship and freedom registers to trace families through several generations. Fortunately, freemen's registers frequently record both masters and parents, making them easier to use for this purpose.

Some apprentices who actually became freemen cannot be traced due to defects in the registration process. The registers do not necessarily record everything that they should have recorded. The minutes and order books of urban courts and assemblies frequently emphasise the need to keep proper records. They would not have done so if proper records were being kept.

The need for proper record keeping was emphasised by the fact that some applicants for the freedom had to be rejected. At Newcastle upon Tyne, an apprentice's name had to be 'called' on three successive guild days. It was open to both his master, and to the steward of his Company, to object to his admission[166]. Some cities kept records of apprentices who were refused the freedom when they had completed their terms. The *Book of Apprentices rejected as Freemen 1780-1802* in Exeter City Archives[167] lists many rejected applicants. There were a variety of different reasons for rejection. If the terms of the indentures had been infringed in any way, or if they had not been properly made, then the apprentice might not secure the freedom. Entries in the *Book* include the following:

'Badgery, James, by apprentship to Wm Beal Junr whitebread baker. Rejected Augst 18th 1792. Ran away. Bound 22nd Ap 1784. Absent above a week without masters consent'.
'Baker, Wm of Exe Lane joiner app with Geo Baker joiner his father. Rejected July 3d 1802. Indenture not indented'.
Channing, Wm. App to John Larkworthy hornmaker - went to sea sevl months during the term. Rejected July 3d 1802.
Gingham, Richd - by appship - part with Edward Tremlett and residue with Joseph Hillman junr. Rejected October 17th 1791 for marrying before his appship expired'.

CHAPTER NINE
Guild Apprenticeship Records

The records of craft guilds and livery companies, where they survive, include much information on apprenticeship. These guilds should not be confused with the religious guilds which were abolished during the reformation, although they did sometimes support religious activities. The records of Exeter's Incorporation of Weavers, Fullers and Shearmen include minute books, account books, freemen's lists and admission certificates, all of which include information about apprentices[168]. Indentures were deposited in the Company's archives. It is probable that registers of apprentices were also kept, but these have been lost.

Similar documentation is available for guilds in many other cities, and especially in London[169]. London records are mostly now held in London Metropolitan Archives[170], although some are still held by the relevant company. Cliff Webb has indexed the apprenticeship registers of over 40 livery companies; these indexes have been published by the Society of Genealogists[171], and are also available online[172], They may be compared with records relating to the freedom of the city[173].

In the provinces, the proceedings of the Company of Soapmakers of Bristol have been published, and make many references to the admissions of apprentices to the freedom. For example, in 1617, they 'receaved in to our Companie Nicholas Hallinge whoe hath served his aprentiship with Richard Baugh unto sopemakinge and chandlinge, and hath also paid for his income iiis iiiid; more, he doth promise to pay repayrations of the haule whensoever it shalbe required iiis iiiid'[174]. The 'income' was the fee for admittance. Such fees, together with fees for enrolment of indentures, may be recorded in wardens' accounts, quarterage books, and other guild records.

CHAPTER TEN
Registers of Parish Apprentices

P arish apprentices may not have been entered in borough apprenticeship registers. They were sometimes not expected to become freemen. Nevertheless, separate registers were sometimes kept by both borough and parish authorities. The 'poor child register' of Southampton for 1609-19 has been published[175]. In Colyton (Devon), a register of apprentices survives from 1598 to 1711[176].

An act of 1766 required parishes in London and Middlesex to maintain registers of apprentices bound by the parish. This act was emulated by an act of 1802, which required the overseers of every parish to keep similar registers. These were to give the names, sex, ages and parents of apprentices. They also name masters, their trades and their residences, stating the premium paid and the term of the apprenticeship. The names of overseers, and of the Justices of the Peace, who gave their assent to the binding, are also given. A book of printed forms was frequently used. Parish apprenticeship registers sometimes provide more information than indentures. They include the names of parents, which were excluded from indentures. Many parish apprenticeship registers have been published by Devon Family History Society[177]. Some for Somerset and Dorset are available online in the 'FFHS Other Records Collection 1320-1996' at

www.findmypast.com. Indexes to 'Staffordshire Apprenticeship Records', 1600-1900 are available at **www.staffsnameindexes.org.uk**.

In 1844, parishes ceased to have power to bind apprentices. Parish apprenticeship registers were closed, and the power of binding was transferred to the guardians of poor law unions. The Apprentices Act 1851 required them to keep registers of apprentices. Surviving Poor Law Union registers are listed by Gibson[178], and record the name of the child, the age, the 'date of hiring or taking as servant', and the name, trade and residence of the master. Sometimes more information than this is given. The Leicester Union register also includes details of parents and their residences, the term of the apprenticeship and the premium paid[179].

CHAPTER ELEVEN
Charity Records

Apprentices bound by charities can frequently be identified in the apprenticeship registers of borough, guild, and parish. Some charities also kept their own records, which can sometimes be found amongst parish and borough records. Charities which had no connection with local government authorities have sometimes deposited their records in local record offices. The register of the Wiltshire Society has already been mentioned. The London Foundling Hospital's records are deposited with the London Metropolitan Archives. They are voluminous, and include minutes of governors' proceedings, registers of apprentices and testimonials. The latter are particularly valuable[180]. The Hospital offered its apprentices a gratuity on completion of their term. This had to be applied for by submitting a testimonial from their master. These testimonials survive and are invaluable character portraits of apprentices and their relationships with their masters.

47

CHAPTER TWELVE
Inland Revenue Apprenticeship Books

The Stamp Duty Act of 1709 imposed a duty on apprenticeship indenture premiums, at 6d in the pound on premiums of £50 or less, and one shilling in the pound on premiums in excess of that amount. Indentures entered into by parochial authorities and by charities, were exempt. So were trades which had not existed when the Statute of Artificers was passed in 1563. The duty was abolished in 1804, but the last payments were not made until 1811.

Registers were kept to record the amounts paid. These are held by the National Archives, class IR 1[181]. The 79 volumes (including some index volumes) are available on microfilm. They record the name, abode, and occupation of the master, the name of the apprentice (and, up to 1752, the name, place of abode and employment, of his father or guardian), the date of the indentures, the date duty was paid, the starting date of the apprenticeship, details of any transfer or assignment of the indentures and the premium paid. After 1760, the amount of information given decreases. In some cases all that is recorded is the amount of duty paid by a particular master, without even the name of the apprentice.

| 54/23 | 1760 | PAGEL(L) | Wm to Rob Mulley of Diss Norf peruk £10 |

PAG(G)ET(T) PAGIT(T) PACHIT PADGET(T)

52/51	1754	Pagell	Jn to Jas Brown of Glasgow comb £8
7/59	1718	Pagett	Abra Wm of Rugby gent to Thos Truesdale of Stamford Lincs gent £68 5/
5/16	1716		Ambr Abra of Leicester gent to Jn Manchester cit & clock £10
13/84	1732	Paget	Chas Jn of Egham Surr to Jos Southam cit & dist £84
22/140	1760	Pagett	Chas to Edw Stevens of St Geo Westr shoe £10
43/118	1714		Dan Joseph of Naveby Leics yeo to Ben Sutton of Loughboro Leics tallch roper & flxd £15
8/71	1720	Paggett	Edw Jn of Mortlake Surr to Letitia Geddings cit & coop £12 10/
51/274	1752	Padget	Edw to Jas Bennet of Bromsgrove merc £6
48/98	1724	Pagett	Edw Geo decd to Dan Hopkins of Oldswinford Glos tay £10
15/67	1737	Padget	Geo Geo of Knighton on Team Worcs to Ric Mound of Neen Sollers Salop shoe £5

3. Page of abstracts from Apprentices of Great Britain 1710-1774. www.originsnetwork.com/help/aboutbo-appgb.aspx, based on the Stamp Duty Registers in the National Archives, IR1/13/84. Note the entry for Chas Paget of Egham, 1732. See also illus. 4 & 5.

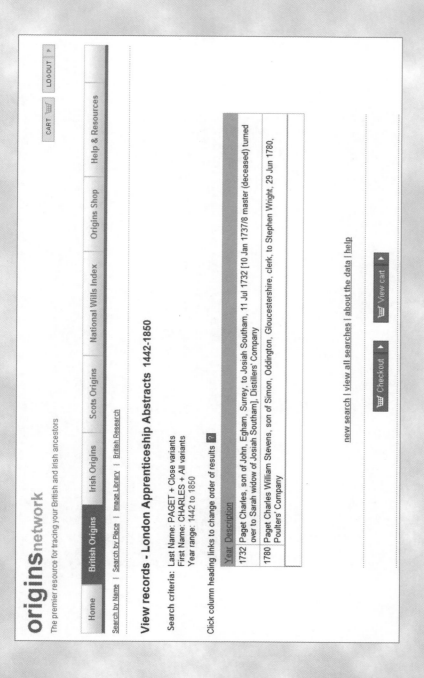

4. The entry for Chas Paget (see illus 3) in London Apprenticeship Abstracts 1442-1850: **www.originsnetwork.com/help/aboutbo-lonapps.aspx**. This is an abstract from the London Distillers Company apprenticeship registers.

5. Apprenticeship indenture for Charles Paget, held in the Crisp & Clench collection by the Society of Genealogists.

There may be marginal annotations, indicating, for example, that part of the premium was paid by a charity, and was therefore exempt, or that the premium was estimated. These registers are in two series. City registers record duty paid in London (which may include duty paid by country masters who went to London to pay). They are arranged chronologically, by the dates on which entries were made, commencing in October 1711. The country registers were compiled from batches of indentures sent up to London by district collectors to be stamped. They are arranged chronologically by collection area, commencing in May 1710.

Some registers are missing, including the earliest city register for 1710-11. Entries could be made some time after the indentures were made, so registers covering a particular period frequently had entries for indentures made several years earlier. For example, Elizabeth Nye's indentures were dated 24th February 1707/8, but duty was not paid until 14th September 1720.

Over 250,000 apprentices are recorded in the surviving registers between 1710 and 1762. There was considerable under-registration. Only a fifth of London's apprentices are recorded in the registers[182]. Evasion in London was a serious problem. It is likely that it was even more serious in rural areas. Legislation dealing with it was passed in 1710, 1719, 1745, 1747, and 1758.

A number of abstracts from the Inland Revenue registers have been published by local record societies. These cover Lincolnshire, Surrey, Sussex, Warwickshire and Wiltshire[183]. An online database is available for Cambridgeshire for 1763-1811[184].

Abstracts of the registers for 1710-1774 are also available at the Society of Genealogists. These abstracts are now online, but the automated indexing is rudimentary. Searching for a particular name will lead you to the page where the name should appear, but only if it is in the database[185]. Visit:

- Apprentices of Great Britain 1710-1774
  www.origins.net/help/popup-aboutbo-appgb.htm

A microfiche edition of these abstracts for the period 1710 to 1762 has been published:

- *Unpublished finding aids for genealogical research, series two: The Society of Genealogists apprenticeship index*. 138 fiche. Harvester Press Microform, 1985.

An unpublished fiche available at the National Archives, the Society of Genealogists, and Guildhall Library, carries this index up to 1774. For the period after 1774, the National Archives holds incomplete indexes to masters only in IR1/76-79.

CHAPTER THIRTEEN

Churchwardens and Overseers Accounts, Minutes and Reports

Churchwardens and overseers were given important roles in the binding of parish apprentices by Elizabethan and later statutes. That role is reflected in their minutes, reports and accounts. Minutes reveal their policies towards apprentices and may include much valuable information about individuals. Reports may reveal the conditions in which apprentices worked, especially in factories. Accounts detail income and expenditure, and may show when costs were incurred on apprenticeship matters[186].

Overseers had to pay for the writing of indentures, the provision of clothing and other incidental expenses. They also had to pay premiums to masters. For example, the Cratfield (Suffolk) churchwardens laid out £1 for 'Hartlates boye for clothes when he went to prentiz' in 1651, and £3 was 'laid out for the bynding of Mynggyes boy' in 1656[187]. The overseers' accounts for Wheatley (Oxfordshire) in 1648 record the payment of 1/- 'for makinge the indentures for Venetia Morris'[188].

Overseers could regain some of their costs by levying fines on masters who refused to accept apprentices, under an act of 1696. The fine for refusal was £10. Payment of the fine came to be seen as a means of purchasing

exemption from the requirement to take an apprentice, as well as a useful supplementary source of income for overseers[189]. There were 352 payments for exemption in Leeds, 1801-1808[190]. The parish of Halifax raised between £100 and £150 from such fines[191].

Churchwardens' accounts are frequently to be found amongst parish records in local record offices. Early accounts are listed by Hutton[192], although it is probable that more could be found. Many have been published by record societies and others.

CHAPTER FOURTEEN
Settlement Examinations

The concept of settlement was fundamental to the operation of the Poor Law. Relief was given by parishes, and, later, by unions, to paupers who were 'settled' in their areas. The place of settlement had to be determined before a pauper could be given relief. If there was doubt, the pauper had to be examined before a Justice of the Peace. The examination was recorded, and the pauper was removed to his place of settlement. Settlement examinations provide mini-biographies of the poor. Apprenticeship gave them the right of settlement, and consequently it is frequently mentioned. For example, in 1751, Anne Piper was examined, and said that 'at the age of about 13 years she was bound an apprentice by the parish officers of Chelsea to one Mary Perry, a milk woman in Charles Street in the parish of St. Margaret Westminster ... until she should attain the age of 21 ... And says that she continued and served her said mistress until she died, which was about a year after she this examinant was bound. And that afterwards she continued with her said mistress's two daughters at the same place ... for about eighteen weeks, but having been (she says) ill-used by their milk carrier she absconded ...'[193]. The examination of Jonathan Taylor in 1820 records that he 'was apprenticed by the parish officers of Leigh to Thomas Andrews of Tewkesbury, cloth weaver, for 7 years, and served the whole time'[194].

Settlement examinations can be found amongst parish, union and quarter session records in local record offices. A few collections have been published by local record societies. Many more are calendared on A2A:

www.nationalarchives.gov.uk/a2a.

CHAPTER FIFTEEN

Quarter Sessions & other Court Records

The Statute of Artificers and Apprentices 1563 gave Justices of the Peace authority to make annual inquiry into the operation of apprenticeship legislation and to deal with complaints made by masters and apprentices. They also, of course, exercised criminal and civil jurisdiction in the counties. Quarter Sessions and Assize proceedings frequently record their activities in dealing with apprentices. In 1679, for example, the minutes of Wiltshire sessions record 'John Williams being now eight yeres of age and lefte by some unknowen beggar within the parishe of Braddford was appointed by the parisshioners to serve Robert Brouncker of Broughton Gyfford, wever, to serve him according to the statute untyll he comme to thage of xxii yeres'[195].

Assize judges sometimes dealt with apprenticeship matters, instructing Justices of the Peace on how they should proceed. In 1642, Robert Foster, Chief Justice of the Common Pleas, heard the case of Elizabeth Clarke, who had refused to take a nine-year old girl on the grounds of her own poverty and the child's incapacity. He instructed the 'two next Justices of the Peace ... doe take the said busines into their examinacion and free the said Elizabeth of the said apprentice if they finde the said informacion to be true'[196].

Justices' note books are the private records of individual justices, and are occasionally found amongst collections of estate and personal papers. Where they are available, they may be very useful. Most disputes between master and servant came first to an individual justice, who was frequently able to decide the case himself without reference to Quarter Sessions. Some justices kept notebooks recording the cases that came before them. The mid-eighteenth century notebook of Edmund Tew is full of references to apprenticeship disputes. In 1751, he wrote to a Sunderland shipbuilder in response to the complaint of eight of his apprentices of 'want of victuals'. When Thomas Maslett, 'a noted perjured youth', absconded from the service of his master, Tew granted a warrant against him. In 1757, he granted a warrant against Michael Dryden's master for 'cruel usage'[197].

For London and Middlesex, the Old Bailey exercised a similar jurisdiction to Quarter Sessions. Its *proceedings* are available online **www.oldbaileyonline.org**, and include many references to apprentices and how they were treated. Masters were frequently treated leniently by the bench, as is illustrated in the case of William Ward:

> 'Edward Sea, of the parish of Edmunton, in the County of Middlesex, was indicted for killing William Ward his apprentice with a horse whip, on the 29th of April last, by striking him over the head three several times. The evidence against the prisoner, deposed that he coming into the work-room (being a silk stoking weaver) he asked the boy when he had cleaned his frame, and the deceased answered at Easter, at which he struck him as afore-said, after which he died within the space of half an hour; but there being several chirugeons which viewed and searched the head of the deceased, and attested that they could not find any cause of his death to proceed from the blow, but rather looked upon it to be some violent fit; and the prisoner having almost twenty credible witnesses to attest that he was no ways given to passion, or that he ever beat any servant unlawfully, he was acquitted'.

Many boroughs had their own courts. Their court books record similar cases. Sometimes, they also record enrolments. In 1621, the Woodstock court book noted that 'John Hiorne places himself apprentice to Robert Spittle of Woodstock, smith and farrier, for the term of seven years'[198].

Sometimes, witness depositions were recorded in separate books. These written statements can be quite detailed, and offer a flavour of the life of the times which can be of great value to the researcher. Depositions relating to the theft of a pair of shoes in Southampton in 1633 reveal an apprentice, John Enough, looking after his master's shop, bargaining with a customer over the price of a pair of shoes, and pursuing the customer when he discovered that she had stolen another pair[199].

The church had its own courts[200]. These had no jurisdiction over the relationship between master and apprentice, but apprentices are frequently mentioned in depositions[201].

Quarter Sessions, borough court, and church court records are held by local record offices. A wide variety of records are held, but legal cases affecting apprentices are likely to be recorded in minute and order books, in depositions and in other records of proceedings. Apprenticeship indentures may also sometimes be found. A brief introduction to the use of Quarter Sessions records is provided by Ratcliffe[202]. A detailed listing is provided by Gibson[203], who also notes a number of published editions.

CHAPTER SIXTEEN
Wills

Wills are a major source of genealogical information, which may record incidental information about apprenticeship. Apprentices sometimes received legacies in their masters' wills. In 1540, an unidentified London widow gave her apprentice, Richarde Shammon, his indentures with liberty to choose another master. She also gave him her shop rent-free for a year, and all of her tools. If he had served his term, her executor was 'to cause the said Richarde to be made free and admytted unto the lyberties of the Citie of London'[204]. William Trotter of Lincoln gave his apprentice, another William Trotter, his 'marbyll jaket' and 'of every tole one belongyng to my occupacion'[205]. Testators sometimes left legacies to provide apprenticeship premiums for their children, or to establish them in business once they had completed their indentures. Many apprenticeship charities were based on the wills of benefactors. Nathaniel Mill, for example, left a substantial legacy 'towards the yearly placing of fower poore mens sonns apprentices that can read and write to some handycraft trade or other trade at the discretion of the Mayor of this towne'[206].

Before 1858, wills were mostly proved in ecclesiastical courts, and many survive in the records of those courts. Gibson & Churchill have provided the authoritative listing of surviving records[207]. A detailed guide to their use is provided by Grannum & Taylor[208].

CHAPTER SEVENTEEN
Poll Books

Poll books record the names of those who voted in Parliamentary elections. In Parliamentary boroughs, the franchise was frequently (but not always) exercised by freemen. Where that was the case, poll books provide lists of the freemen who cast their vote. Many of them, of course, were freemen by virtue of their apprenticeship.

Poll books can be found in many libraries and record offices. There are major collections at the Institute of Historical Research and the British Library. A full listing is provided by Gibson & Rogers[209].

CHAPTER EIGHTEEN
Parliamentary Papers

The Parliamentary papers provide a mass of evidence relating to apprenticeship. The reports of the Charity Commission, for example, identify many apprenticeship charities. The Poor Law Commission's *Report on the employment of women and children in agriculture* (1843), includes evidence from the South West on the practice of apprenticing pauper children. This includes some evidence from apprentices themselves, giving details of their lives. The *Report* of the Royal Commission on Childrens Employment in Mines and Mining (1843) also includes evidence provided by apprentices themselves. Joan Lane's study of Warwickshire cotton mill apprentices is based on a select committee report[210]. A useful list of reports and papers relating to apprentices is given by Dunlop[211]. Reference may also be made to Cockton's catalogue[212], and to the Bopcris website[213]. Parliamentary papers can be found in most large reference libraries, and a database is also available online. Free online access may be available in University libraries.

CHAPTER NINETEEN
Newspapers

Newspapers carrying advertisements began to be popular in the late eighteenth century. As early as 1779, the Bristol Corporation of the Poor ordered a committee to 'take into consideration the putting out the children apprentice, and advertise the same in the papers as they shall think necessary'[214]. They also used newspapers to advertise the punishment inflicted on a master who had misbehaved towards a girl apprentice[215]. Newspapers frequently carried advertisements from masters seeking apprentices, and from parents seeking masters. In 1799, for example, the *Coventry Mercury* carried an advertisement for 'An apprentice wanted by a surgeon and apothecary in good business. A youth, properly educated, may meet with a situation attended by peculiar advantages. He will be treated as one of the family. An adequate premium will therefore be required'[216]. Poor law authorities placed similar advertisements. The *Exeter Flying Post* for 5th January 1792 carried an advertisement from the overseers of Kenwyn (Cornwall). They had four children aged 10 to 15, who they would 'bind out with suitable premiums to any persons of good character who carry on trades whereby the said apprentices my be enabled to get their livings'[217].

Masters also advertised for the return of runaway apprentices. Sometimes they really did want them back, but frequently the advertisement was a matter of form, placed in order to disclaim any liability for their apprentice's actions. Cornelius Brinkley, for example, absconded in 1780 from Dr. Green of Plymouth. An advertisement was placed in the *Exeter Flying Post* on 25th August 1780, stating that he was thought to be 'lurking in the neighbourhood of Exeter or Cullompton. No reward will be given for apprehending him, but his master will be obliged to any press gang that will lay hold of him'[218].

Very few newspapers are currently indexed. However, the British Library has digitised over 2,000,000 pages from 49 different newspapers[219], and is intending to digitise more. Its database is easy to search online. It does make a small charge, but many public libraries have subscribed to it, making the database freely available through their websites. The *Times* is also fully digitised, and frequently available through public library websites. A full listing of newspapers is provided by Gibson, et al[220].

CHAPTER TWENTY
Acts of Parliament & other Legislation

A pprentices have been the subject of much legislation, from the medieval period onwards. Many of the records that have been described above have been initiated by, or conform to, Acts of Parliament. Researchers need to be aware of this legislation, and of how it has affected record keeping. The more important statutes are listed below, with notes and some abstracts[221].

Statute of Canterbury 1388/9 (12 Ric. II, c5)

The fourteenth-century Parliament primarily consisted of manorial lords, who were suffering from the lack of labour after the Black Death. Many of their workers were migrating to the towns, where their children were sometimes apprenticed. This Act banned the practice of apprenticing the children of rural labourers:

> 'It is ordained and assented that he or she which use to labour at the plough and cart, or other labour or service of husbandry, till they be of the age of twelve years, that from thenceforth they shall abide at the same labour, without being put to any mystery or handicraft; and if any covenant or bond of apprentice be from henceforth made to the contrary, the same shall be holden for none'.

Apprentices' Act 1405/6 (7 Henry IV, c.17)

This statute modified the statute of 1388/9, which was not being properly observed. Children of rural labourers were still being 'bound apprentices to divers crafts within the cities and boroughs of the ... Realm... so that there is so great scarcity of labourers and other servants of husbandry, that the gentlemen and other people of the realm be greatly impoverished'. The law was therefore tightened up. The parents of apprentices had to be able to show that they had lands valued at £1 per annum at least. A certificate from two Justices of the Peace, confirming the value of their land, had to be presented to the authorities of the borough where their child was to be apprenticed.

Bodies Incorporate Act 1503 (19 Henry VII, c.7)

Craft guilds were forbidden to make by-laws without the approval of the Lord Chancellor, or of the judges of central or assize courts. This reduced their ability to make ordinances affecting apprentices.

Apprentices Act 1530 (22 Henry VIII, c.4)

This Act limited the fees of apprentices for entry to guilds to 2s 6d, and the fees for entering the freedom of cities to 3s 6d. Guilds frequently circumvented the rules by asking candidates for a 'voluntary' contribution towards the repair of their hall, the maintenance of almsmen, or some other purpose supported by the guild[222].

Apprentices Act 1536 (28 Henry VIII, c.5)

This Act reinforced the Act of 1530, which guilds had tried to circumvent by making apprentices take oaths to pay fees for their freedom when they were bound. Guilds were forbidden to extract oaths from apprentices in this way.

Punishment of Vagabonds Act 1547 (1 Edward VI, c.3)

In the opinion of Edward VI's Parliament, the young children of beggars, if 'brought up in idleness, might be so rooted in it that hardly they may be brought after to good thrift and labour'. Legislation was therefore passed to allow masters to apprehend such children, and to bring them before constables and Justices of the Peace. These officers were authorised to bind such children apprentices until the age of 24 for boys, or 21 for girls, to the person who apprehended them. If the child ran away, the master could 'punish the said child in chains or otherwise', and treat him or her as his slave. Parents could not intervene in the legal process of binding.

Statute of Artificers & Apprentices, 1563 (5 Eliz I, c.4.)

This statute replaced all previous legislation on apprenticeship, and provided its legal basis for over 250 years. It contained 'divers orders for artificers, labourers, servants of husbandry and apprentices', and aimed to 'banish idleness, advance husbandry, and yeild unto the hired person ... a convenient proportion of wages'. It expected everyone to be an apprentice, and required the 'custom of London' to be observed throughout the realm. It laid down that:

> 'every person, being an housholder, and having and using half a plough-lande at the least in tillage, maye have and receive as an apprentice any person above the age of ten years, and under the age of eighteen years, to serve in husbandry, until his age of one and twenty years at the least, or until the age of twenty-four years as the parties can agree, and the said retainer and taking of an apprentice to be made and done by indenture'.

Hitherto, apprenticeship had been an urban institution. This Act extended its scope in order to provide a means of social control over young rural labourers. Such labourers were still, however, denied the right to be apprenticed in towns and cities.

In the towns, the right to be a master was given to 'every person being an housholder, and twenty-four years old at the least, dwelling ... in any city or town corporate, and using and exercising any art, mystery or manual occupation there'. Such people were permitted to 'have and retain the son of any freeman not occupying husbandry nor being a labourer, and inhabiting in the same or in any other city or town ... incorporate, to serve and be bound as an apprentice after the custom and order of the City of London for seven years at the least'.

Seven years became the normal term of service, although subsequent acts required pauper children to serve for much longer. The reference to the 'custom of the City of London' is important for researchers. That custom included the enrolment of indentures in registers or other records. Such enrolment was not, however, directly mentioned in the Act, and no provision was made for its implementation. It is not surprising that there were many complaints that enrolments were not being made[223]. However, the requirement for indentures probably was generally complied with. They are now a major source of information on apprenticeship, although many have been lost.

Government left it to the guilds, and to borough authorities, to administer the Act. Its effectiveness depended on their diligence or negligence. The statute merely specified who could be master, and who could be apprenticed. Merchants, for example, were forbidden 'to take any apprentice or servante to be instructed ...

except such servante or apprentice be his son, or else that the father or mother of such apprentice or servant shall have ... landes tenementes or other hereditaments of the clear yearly value of forty shillinges'. This had to be certified 'under the hands and seals of three Justices of the Peace ... to the mayor, bailiff, or other head officer of such city or town corporate, and to be inrolled among the records ther'. Other urban dwellers 'not occupying husbandry nor being a labourer', could 'have in like manner to apprentice or apprentices, the child or children of any other artificer or articers not occupying husbandry nor being a laborer'.

No restriction was placed on admission to rural trades. Anyone 'using or exercising the art or occupation of a smith, wheel-wright, plough-wright, mill-wright, carpenter, rough mason, plaisterer, sawyer, lime-burner, brick-maker, bricklayer, tyler, slater, helier, tyle-maker, linen-weaver, turner, cooper, millers, earthen potters, wollen weaver, weaving huswives, or houshold cloth only and none other, clothe, fuller otherwise called tucker or walker, burner of oare and wood ashes, thatcher or shingler' could 'wheresover he or they shall dwell ... have or receive the son of any person as apprentice ... albeit the father or mother or any such apprentice have not any landes tenements nor hereditaments'. However, apprentices of woollen cloth weavers had to have parents whose lands were valued at £3 per annum.

The importance that Parliament attached to apprenticeship was emphasised by the clause requiring every tradesman to have served an apprenticeship:

> 'it shall not be lawfull ... to set up occupy use or exercise any craft mystery or occupation now used ... within the realm of England or Wales, excepte he shall have been brought up therin seven years at the least as an apprentice'.

This was backed up by a clause permitting any rural householder of substance to require anyone deemed suitable to become their apprentice in husbandry. If they refused, they could be dragged before a Justice of the Peace:

> 'if any person shall be required by any householder, having and using half a plough-land at the least in tillage, to be an apprentice and to serve in husbandry or in any other kind of art, mystery, or science before expressed, and shall refuse so to do, that then, upon the complaint of such housekeeper made to one Justice of the Peace ... they shall have full power and authority by virtue hereof, to send for the same person so refusing [and] to commit him unto ward, there to remain until he be contented and will bee bounden to serve as an apprentise shoulde serve'.

The Act did make some provision for the rights of apprentices and other servants. Apprentices could complain against their masters. So could masters against their apprentices.

'If any such master shall misuse or evil intreat his apprentice, or that the said apprentice shall have any just cause to complain, or the apprentice do not his duty to his master, then the said master or apprentice being grieved and having cause to complain shall repair unto one Justice of Peace within the said county, or to the mayor ... , who shall by his wisdom and discretion take such order and direction between the said master and his apprentice as the equity of the cause shall require'.

Apprentices could be freed from their indentures if their masters treated them badly, but they could also be subjected to 'due correction and punishment' if they offended. Those who absconded could be imprisoned.

It is doubtful whether the provisions of the Act were effectively enforced during Elizabeth's reign. In 1606 a complaint was made that the Act 'was made difficult and evaded'[224]. A petition to the Privy Council in the same year complained that in some places no provision was being made for the enrolment of indentures, and that Justices of the Peace were neglecting their statutory duty of making annual inquiry into offences against this Act. It was only after this petition that the Southampton register of apprentices was commenced[225]. The Act was repealed in 1814, but had been increasingly obsolete in many respects, since it was held to apply only to occupations which had existed in 1563.

Poor Law Acts 1597 & 1601 (39 Eliz I, c.3, & 43 Eliz I, c.2.)

The Elizabethan gentry and aristocracy were obsessed by the fear of swarming masses of beggars. This fear was expressed in legislation, most notably in the Poor Law Acts of 1597 and 1601. These Acts established that parishes were responsible for the relief of the poor. They created the post of parish overseer of the poor, and gave overseers and churchwardens power to apprentice poor children (not just paupers). Apprenticeship premiums could be paid from a parish rate. The maximum age at which a parish child could be bound was set at 14. A boy was to serve until the age of 24, a girl until 21 or earlier marriage.

'It shall be lawfull for the said churchwardens & overseers ... by the assent of any two Justices of the Peace, to bind any such children ... to be apprentices, where they shall see convenient, till such man child shall come to the age of four and twenty years and such woman child to the age of one and twenty yeares [the 1601 Act adds 'or the time of her marriage']: the same to be as effectuall to all purposes as if such child were of full age and by indenture of covenant bound him or her selfe'.

Charitable Funds Act 1610 (7 Jas I, c.3)

Many charities had been founded to fund the binding of apprentices in the sixteenth century. This Act encouraged benefactors to place their funds in the care of urban corporations or, in the case of rural parishes, clergy and parish officers, they to have 'the nomination and placing of such apprentices, and the guiding and employment of all such monies'.

Book of Orders 1631

The administration of the poor law acts of 1597 and 1601 was fraught with difficulties, and therefore received attention when the government of Charles I issued its instructions to Justices of the Peace in 1631. The *book of orders* directed that 'the poore children in every parish be put forth apprentices to husbandry and other handy-crafts; and money to be raised in the parishes for placing them, according to the law; and if any party shall refuse to take the said apprentice, being put out according to the law, such party as shall refuse to take the said apprentice to be bound over to the next quarter sessions and there to be bound to his good behaviour, or otherwise ordered, as shall be found fit.'[226].

Act of Settlement 1662 (13 & 14 Car. II, c.12)

The Acts of 1597 and 1601 had made poor relief the responsibility of the parish. However, overseers were only responsible for their own poor. 'By reason of some defects in the Law', they could not restrain the poor 'from going from one parish to another 'endeavouring' to settle themselves in those parishes where there is the best stock, the largest commons or wastes to build cottages and the most woods for them to burn and destroy, and when they have consumed it then to another parish and at last become rogues and vagabonds to the great discouragement of parishes to provide stocks where it is liable to be devoured by strangers'. This Act gave Justices of the Peace the authority to prevent this happening. 'Upon complaint made by the churchwardens or overseers of the poor of any Parish to any Justice of Peace within forty days after any such person or persons coming so to settle as aforesaid in any tenement under the yearly value of ten pounds' two Justices of the Peace together could remove any person 'likely to be chargeable to the parish', and order their conveyance 'to such parish where he or they were last legally setled either as a native householder sojourner apprentice or servant for the space of forty days at the least, unless he or they give sufficient security for the discharge of the said parish'. This clause implied that apprentices had the right of settlement in the parish where their master lived.

Act of Settlement 1691 (3 William & Mary, c.11)

The implication of the Act of 1602 had to be clarified by this Act, which confirmed that 'if any person shall be bound an apprentice by indenture and inhabit in any town or parish, such binding and inhabitation shalt be adjudged a good settlement.'

Act for Relief of the Orphans and other Creditors of the City of London. 1694 (5 &6 William & Mary, c.3)

In 1694, the City of London was in financial difficulties. The funds of the city's orphans, which had been deposited with the City authorities for safe keeping, had been used for municipal purposes, and could not be repaid. This Act set out to remedy the situation. It imposed a tax of 2s 6d on the binding of all apprentices within the City, to be collected by the master or warden of each livery company. They were to:

'provide and keep in their common halls one or more book or books of vellum or parchment in which every such sum of two shillings and six pence shall be set down and entered by the said master or wardens or their respective deputy or deputies, and the name of the apprentice who paid the same'.

Poor Relief Act 1696 (8 & 9 Will. III, c.30.

The apprenticeship of pauper children under the acts of 1597 and 1601 had encountered some difficulties, so much so that Lord Keeper Coventry had charged the judges that 'a strict course be taken against them that oppose it'[227]. This Act confirmed that masters could be compelled to accept pauper apprentices, or be fined £10 for refusing to do so.

Sea Apprentices Act 1703 (2 & 3 Anne, c.6)

This Act made provision for pauper children aged 10 or over to be apprenticed to the masters of sailing ships until they were 21. The premium was to be 50/-, and clothing was to be provided. Apprentices could not be pressed for the Royal Navy until they were 18. Masters and owners were required to accept at least one apprentice each, depending on the size of their ships. Collectors of customs in each port were to enrol the indentures, and to certify details (including the names of ships) to the Admiralty. They were also required to keep registers of every ship which called at their ports; masters had to report to them the names of each apprentice on board. Their registers recorded the names of ships, masters and apprentices, and had to identify the parishes from which apprentices came. Copies of these registers were to be deposited with Quarter Sessions and borough archives.

Stamp Duty Act 1709 (8 Anne c.9.)

This Act imposed a duty on premiums 'given paid contracted or agreed for with or in relation to every Clerk Apprentice or servant ... to learn any Profession, Trade or Employmen'. The sum demanded was 6d in the pound on amounts of under £50, and one shilling in the pound on premiums of over £50, with effect from 1st May 1710. Indentures were required to state the premium paid, and were 'hereby required to be stamped' by newly appointed Commissioners of Stamp Duty. If produced in London, they were to be immediately stamped. If produced to local collectors, they were to be receipted by them, and sent up to London in batches to be stamped. This Act was made perpetual in 1710, and repealed in 1804. Rice's edition of the Sussex entries[228] includes a useful introduction to the legislation.

Servants & Apprentices Act 1747 (20 Geo II, c.19)

This Act permitted apprentices, whose premiums were under £5 (i.e. predominantly pauper apprentices) to complain to JPs about their 'misusage, refusal of necessary provision, cruelty or other ill-treatment'. Masters could also complain about apprentice's misbehaviour, and used this Act to dismiss them.

Rates & Duties Act 1757 (30 Geo.II, c.19.)

Indentures could be 'ingrossed, written, or printed', provided that they were stamped. Henceforth, apprenticeship agreements were frequently made on printed forms.

Apprentices Act 1765 (6 Geo.III, c.25)

Absconding apprentices were a serious problem. This Act laid down that 'if any apprentice shall absent himself from his master's service before the term of his apprenticeship shall be expired, every such apprentice shall ... whenever he shall be found, be compelled to serve his said master for so long a time as he shall have absented himself ...'.

Parish Poor Children Act 1766 (7 George III, c.39)

The care of poor children in London was regulated by this Act, which included provision for binding them as apprentices. It limited the term of servitude to seven years or age 21, and set a minimum premium of £4 2s, payable in installments. It also provided for the maintenance of registers of poor children and of apprentices, to be kept in every parish in London and Middlesex. Apprentice registers kept under this Act give details of both apprentices and their masters, and record premiums paid.

Parish Apprentices Act, 1778 (18 Geo. III, c.47)

The Act of 1766 had reduced the term of service for an apprentice in London to age 21. This Act extended that provision to the whole of England and Wales.

Parish Apprentices Act 1780 (20 Geo. III, c.36)

Not unnaturally, many masters objected to being required to accept pauper children as apprentices. The legality of this requirement had been brought into question despite the Act of 1696. This Act clarified the law by insisting that masters 'to whom any poor children shall be appointed to be bound apprentice', were 'hereby required to receive and provide for such children'. This only applied to masters who were resident in the apprentice's parish of settlement.

Chimney Sweeps Act 1788 (28 Geo. III, c.48)

The intention of this Act was to 'prevent various complicated miseries, to which boys employed in climbing and cleansing of chimneys are liable'. Churchwardens and overseers could only bind children aged 8 or over to a chimney sweep. Servitude was to last only until age 16. No sweep could have more than 6 apprentices at any one time, or hire them out to any other master. A set form of indenture was prescribed; amongst other things, this required masters to ensure that apprentices were 'thoroughly washed and cleaned from soot and dirt at least once a week'. They had to provide clothing suitable both for their work and for attendance at church.

Parish Apprentices Act 1792 (32 Geo. III, c.57.)

The indentures of parish apprentices whose masters had died were to expire three months after the death (provided that the premium had been under £5). Justices of the Peace were given authority to re-assign those apprentices whose masters had died. They could also discharge apprentices if their master had 'become insolvent, or is so far reduced in his or her circumstances as to be unable to employ or maintain such apprentices'. Masters who had been compelled to accept parish apprentices could also re-assign them to other masters with the consent of magistrates.

Fines on Parish Officers and Masters of Apprentices Act 1793 (33 Geo.III, c.55)

Concern at the ill-treatment of apprentices prompted this Act. It argued that 'it is ... expedient to impower justices to impose fines upon masters of apprentices for ill usage of such apprentices', and set a maximum penalty of £2.

Desertion of Seamen Act 1796 (37 George III, c.73)

The aim of this Act was 'to prevent the desertion of seamen from British ships trading to ... The West Indies'. It required masters of ships of over 100 tons to have on board at least one apprentice aged under 17. Indentures were to be enrolled at Customs Houses, and apprentices were to serve for 3 years. They were exempt from service in the Royal Navy.

Registration of Pauper Apprentices Act 1802 (42 Geo III, c.46)

By this Act, parish overseers were required to maintain a register of children bound by them as apprentices. The form of the register has already been discussed. These registers are valuable sources for family historians; indeed, they are more useful than indentures, since they record details of parents.

Health and Morals of Apprentices Act 1802 (42 Geo.III, c.73)

This Act noted that 'it hath of late become a common practice in cotton and woollen mills, and in cotton and woollen factories, to employ a great number of male and female apprentices and other persons in the same building'. It had therefore 'become necessary to preserve the health and morals of such apprentices and other persons' by regulation. The Act laid down that the working day in such places was not to exceed 12 hours, and that all-night working was to be ended. Masters were required to ensure that apprentices were taught reading, writing and arithmetic, and religious instruction was to be given on Sundays. There were to be separate sleeping quarters for boys and girls, and no more than 2 children were to sleep in the same bed. Inspectors were to be appointed to enforce the provisions of the Act.

Repeal Act 1814 54 Geo III, c.96

This Act repealed the apprenticeship provisions of the Statute of Artificers 1563. Parts of that Act had long been moribund, or ignored. Inflation had rendered the restriction of apprenticeship to those whose parents had lands valued at over £2 pointless. In 1638, 38 of the 60 boys apprenticed in Oxford were the sons of labourers, contrary to the Act, but typical of normal practice. The Act was held to apply only to occupations which had been in existence in 1563. Repeal was long overdue.

Parish Apprentices Act 1816 (56 George III, c.139)

This Act was designed to remedy the 'many grievances' which had 'arisen from the binding of poor children as apprentices by parish officers to improper persons and to persons residing at a distance, whereby the said parish officers, and the parents of such children, are deprived of the opportunity of knowing the manner in which such children are treated, and the parents and children have in many instances become estranged from each other'. Justices were required to 'enquire into the propriety of binding such child apprentices to the person or persons to whom it shall be proposed by ... overseers to bind such child' especially having regard to the character of the proposed master, and the distance of his residence from the child's parish. They were authorised to consult the child's parents if they wished, but could not normally allow a child to be bound to a master who lived more than 40 miles distant. The Act also banned the apprenticeship of children under nine years of age.

Merchant Seamen Apprentices Act 1823 (4 George IV, c.25)

This Act modified the Act of 1796, and required apprentices to serve for at least four years.

Poor Law Amendment Act 1834 (4 & 5 William IV, c.76)

This Act laid the basis for the administration of the Victorian poor law, but was unenthusiastic about pauper apprenticeship. It removed the powers of parish overseers and Justices of the Peace to bind apprentices, transferring the responsibility to the newly created guardians of poor law unions. The Poor Law Commission was to set regulations for the administration of the system, and Justices of the Peace were to make sure that these regulations were complied with. However, the Poor Law Commission's opinion was 'unfavourable to that state of servitude which is created by the apprenticeship of parish children'[229]. No regulations relating to apprentices were issued until the Act of 1844 was passed.

Merchant Seamen Act 1835 (5 & 6 William IV, c.19)

This Act consolidated the law relating to seamen, and established the General Register Office of Merchant Seamen. It granted overseers and guardians of the poor the power to bind pauper children to the 'sea service'. Such children had to be aged 13 or over, 'of sufficient health and strength', and had to give their consent. They could be bound until age 21. Indentures had to state their age. Apprentices could only be 'turned over' to another master with their consent. Copies of indentures were to be deposited in the local Customs House or, if in the Port of London, with the Registrar. Local customs officers were to keep apprenticeship registers and were to make quarterly returns of entries to the Registrar, who was to keep his own register. Registers were to note dates of indentures, names and ages of apprentices, names and residences of masters and details of the ships on which apprentices served.

Poor Law Amendment Act 1844

This Act gave the Poor Law Commission the power to 'prescribe the duties of the masters to whom poor children may be apprenticed, and the terms and conditions to be inserted in the indentures by which such children may be so bound as apprentices'. Guardians had the power of binding, and were to 'cause all apprentices so bound ... to be registered by their clerk' in accordance with the Act of 1802. Parish apprentices registers ceased, and Poor Law Union registers commenced. Compulsion on masters to accept parish apprentices also ceased.

The Commission did issue regulations under this Act. They banned the binding of children aged under 9 and of children who could not read or write their own name. An apprentice's consent to the binding was required if he was aged 14 or over. The Commissioners were reluctant to allow premiums to be paid, especially for older children, but were forced to give way on this point and were only able to prevent their payment with youths of 17 and over[230].

Poor Law Apprentices Act 1851 (14 & 15 Victoria)

Provision was made by this Act for the 'better protection of persons who are under the care and control of others as apprentices or servants'. Masters who refused or neglected to provide their apprentices with 'necessary food, clothing, or lodging', or who assaulted them, were to be prosecuted.

The Act also required Poor Law guardians to keep a register of everyone under the age of 16 who they sent into service or bound apprentice. Relieving officers were required to visit them twice a year, and to prepare a written report 'whether he has found reason to believe that such young person is not supplied with necessary food, or is subjected to cruel or illegal treatment in any respect'. If a child was placed with a master in another union, then that union's relieving officer was given the duty. Reports of relieving officers may survive amongst Union records.

Merchant Shipping Act 1894 (57 & 58 Victoria)

The indentures of apprentices on fishing boats had to be deposited with the Registrar General of Shipping and Seamen.

CHAPTER TWENTY ONE
Published Sources

Many apprenticeship and freemen's registers, and related sources, have been published. The bibliography which follows is selective, and does not include the many brief lists which appear in family history society journals. Nor does it include the many collections of miscellanea, including apprenticeship records, which have been issued on fiche by family history societies. I have, however, listed a number of general works on apprenticeship which may be of interest to family historians. Much information on apprenticeship is noted incidentally in record publications relating to quarter sessions, proceedings of borough courts, churchwardens' accounts, and other sources. These are not listed here, but some references to them appear in footnotes.

There are many other works on apprenticeship. Numerous brief articles can be found in family history society journals. These were listed in *Family history news and digest*, until that journal ceased publication. They are also listed in the county volumes of my British genealogical library guides. The Royal Historical Society's Bibliography **www.rhs.ac.uk/bibl** lists numerous other books and articles which may be of use.

Most of the works listed here, together with many that are not, may be found in the library of the Society of Genealogists. At the time of writing, no less than 298 titles can be found by searching for 'Apprentices' as a

subject at **www.sog.org.uk/sogcat**. Use the 'look for' box to specify subject. It is also possible to search this catalogue for specific titles. Records relating to particular places can also be found using a subject search.

Many other libraries also hold the titles listed here. Most have catalogues available online. If you have difficulty locating a particular title, you should ask the reference librarian in your local library to suggest where you might find it.

The most important general work on the history of apprenticeship is:

Lane, Joan. *Apprenticeship in England, 1600-1914*. UCL Press, 1996.

See also:

Ben-Amos, Ilana Krausman. *Adolescence and youth in early modern England*. Yale University Press, 1994.

Davies, Margaret Gay. *The enforcement of English apprenticeship: a study in applied mercantilism, 1563-1642*. Harvard University Press, 1956.

Dunlop, Olive Jocelyn. *English apprenticeship and child labour: a history.* T. Fisher Unwin, 1912.

Honeyman, Katrina. *Child workers in England, 1780-1820: parish apprentices and the making of the early industrial labour force*. Studies in labour history. Ashgate, 2007.

Golland, Jim. 'Compell'd to weep: the apprenticeship system', *Genealogists magazine* 23, 1989, p.121-7.

Thomas, E.G. 'Pauper apprenticeship', *Local historian* 14, 1981, p.400-6.

- Apprenticeship of Workhouse Children
  www.workhouses.org.uk/index.html?education/apprenticeship.shtml

For a brief general introduction to apprenticeship records, consult:
- Apprenticeship Records as Sources for Genealogy
  www.nationalarchives.gov.uk/catalogue/RdLeaflet.asp?sLeafletID=295

The majority of the publications listed here are local in character, and are listed by county and place. However, a number relate to particular occupations nation-wide; these are listed first.

Book Trades

Feather, John Pliny. 'Country book trade apprentices, 1710-1760', *Publishing history* 6, 1979, p.85-99. List based on Inland Revenue records.

Maxted, Ian. *The British book trades: 1710-1777: an index of the masters and apprentices recorded in the Inland Revenue registers at the Public Record Office, Kew.* Exeter, 1983.

Clockmakers

Loomes, Brian. *The early clockmakers of Great Britain.* N A G Press, 1981.

Dockyard Apprentices

McGovern, Michael T. *List of workmen & apprentices in His Majesty's dockyards 1748: an alphabetical index transcribed from AD106/2976 at the Public Record Office.* Naval Dockyards Society research series 2. Naval Dockyards Society, 2002

- Sea Your History: Apprentices
  www.seayourhistory.org.uk/content/view/62/146
  Dockyard apprentices in the twentieth century. No names

Electrical Engineers

A register of ex-apprentices & ex-trainees of the Metropolitan-Vickers Electrical Co. Ltd. [1902-56]. 4th ed. Metropolitan-Vickers Electrical Co. Ltd., 1957. 13,000 electrical engineering apprentices trained at Trafford Park, Germiston, Motherwell, and Sheffield.

Emigrant Apprentices

Coldham, Peter Wilson. *Child apprentices in America from Christ's Hospital, London, 1617-1778.* Genealogical Publishing Co., 1990.

Gill, Harold B. *Apprentices of Virginia, 1623-1800.* Ancestry, 1989.

Medical Professions

Wallis, Peter John, & Wallis, R.V. *Eighteenth century medics: subscriptions, licenses, apprenticeships.* 2nd ed. Project for Historical Biography, 1988.

Trawlermen

Wilcox, Martin. 'Opportunity or exploitation? Apprenticeship in the British trawl fisheries, 1850-1936', *Genealogists magazine* 28(4), 2004, p.135-49.

Bedfordshire

Jenkinson, Hilary, Mrs. 'A list of Bedfordshire apprentices', *Bedfordshire Historical Record Society* 9. 1925.

Pickford, Chris. *Bedfordshire clock & watchmakers, 1752-1880*. Bedfordshire Historical Record Society 70. 1991. Includes; 'Bedfordshire clock and watchmaking apprentices: an alphabetical list'.

Berkshire

Hungerford
Bartlett, Eileen, ed. *Hungerford Union Workhouse: workhouse births and deaths 1866-1914; pauper's service book 1877-1917*. Berkshire registers, 2. Eureka Partnership, 2005. List of apprenticeships.

Cambridgeshire

* Cambridgeshire Masters and their Apprentices 1763-1811
  www.cfhs.org.uk/Apprentices/index.html
  Index to 8,194 Cambridgeshire masters and apprentices, from the Inland Revenue apprenticeship books.

Cheshire

Chester
Bennett, J.H.E., ed. *The rolls of the freemen of the City of Chester*. 2 pts. Lancashire and Cheshire Record Society 51 & 55. 1906-8. Pt.1. 1392-1700. Pt.2. 1700-1805.

Cornwall

Cornwall Record Office's Apprentice Index: Apprentices' Index. Cornwall Family History Society, 1992. There is a separate *Masters' Index*.

Derbyshire

Briggs, W. G. 'Records of an apprenticeship charity, 1685-1753', *Journal of the Derbyshire Archaeological & Natural History Society*, 74, 1953, p.43-61.

Devon

Ashton apprentices register, 1804-1841. Devon Family History Society, 2005. There are similar volumes covering *Ashwater, 1803-1831, Awliscombe, 1803-1839, Bere Ferrers, 1805-1817, Bradninch, 1822-1844, Branscombe, 1808-1833, Broadhempston, 1802-1842, Buckfastleigh, 1833-1844, Burlescombe, 1803-1835, Clyst St Mary, 1804-1831, Cockington, 1803-1842, Coffinswell, 1804-1826, Dalwood, 1804-1827, Dawlish, 1833-1834, Dunchideock, 1807-1832, East Budleigh, 1802-1937, Gidleigh, 1803-1841, Gittisham 1803-1838, Harpford, 1804-1839, Holne, 1804-1830, Huntsham 1744-1811, Ide, 1805-1835, Kenton, 1801-1810, 1811-1820, 1821-1830, & 1831-1840, Kingsteignton 1775-1823, Littleham & Exmouth 1800-1834, Luffincott, 1808-1827, Lustleigh, 1803-1833, Lympstone, 1802-1837, Meeth 1803-1840, Modbury, 1833-1839, Payhembury, 1802-1834, Rose Ash, 1803-1844, Seaton & Beer, 1803-1829, Shillingford St George, 1807-1832, Stockland, 1803-1830, Tormoham, 1803-1836, Whitestone 1803-1839 & Withycombe Raleigh, 1800-1834.*

Brixham
Brixham trawler apprentice register 1891-1895. Devon Family History Society, 2005. A further volume covers 1896-1901.

Exeter
Rowe, Margery Mary., & Jackson, Andrew Macpherson, eds. *Exeter freemen, 1266-1967*. Devon & Cornwall Record Society Extra series 1. 1973.

Durham
Evison, Val, ed. *County Durham apprenticeship indentures 1308-1929*. Fiche. Wideopen: Original Indexes, 2001.

Sunderland
Furness, Frederick, & Furness, Moira, eds. *Sunderland apprenticeships, 1781-1900*. Tyne & Wear County Council Archives Department, 1981.

Gloucestershire & Bristol

Bristol
Hollis, D., et al, eds. *Calendar of the Bristol apprentice book, 1532-1565*. 3 vols. Bristol Record Society 14, 33 & 43. 1948-80.

McGregor, Margaret, ed. *Bristol apprentice book*. 4 vols. Bristol & Avon Family History Society, [198-]-1994. Covers 1566-93.

Matthews, Harold Evan, ed. *Proceedings, minutes, and enrolments of the Company of Soapmakers, 1562-1642.* Bristol Record Society 10. 1940.

Butcher, E.E., ed. *The Bristol Corporation of the Poor 1696-1834.* Bristol Record Society 3. 1931.

Gloucester
Barlow, Jill, ed. *A Calendar of the registers of the apprentices of the City of Gloucester, 1595-1700.* Gloucestershire record series 14. Bristol & Gloucestershire Archaeological Society, 2001.

Hampshire

Surry, Nigel. 'Hampshire apprentices to the Painter Stainers Company: their professional activities and social origins, c. 1660-1795', *Proceedings of the Hampshire Field Club and Archaeological Society* 37, 1981, 63-71. Includes list of masters and apprentices, 1660-1795.

Southampton
Willis, Arthur John, & Merson, Allan Leslie, eds. *A calendar of Southampton apprenticeship registers, 1609-1740.* Southampton Records series 12. 1968.

Kent
Bartlett, A E., ed *Kent masters & their apprentices 1763-74.* 2 fiche. Record Publication 24. Kent Family History Society, 1984.

Birchington
Birchington apprenticeship indentures 1633-1838. Fiche. Record publication 856. Kent Family History Society, 1989.

Canterbury
Bartlett, A.E. *Canterbury masters and their apprentices 1763-1777:* with a few entries of 1758-1762. Harrington Family Miscellany Record Publication, 1978.

Cowper, Joseph Meadows. *Canterbury freemen: the roll of the freemen of the city of Canterbury ... from AD 1392-1800.* Fiche. Kent Family History Society, 1999.

Deal
St. Leonard, Deal: apprenticeship indentures, 1661-1788. 10 fiche. Record publication 402. Kent Family History Society, 1986.

Gravesend & Milton

Green, E.R. *Gravesend & Milton masters & apprentices, 1636-1834.* Fiche. Record publication 1860. Kent Family History Society, 1999.

Lancashire

Lancaster

Hughes, Thomas Cann, ed. *The rolls of the freemen of the Borough of Lancaster, 1688 to 1840.* Lancashire & Cheshire Record Society 87 & 90. 1935-8.

Manchester

Hepplewhite, Anne, & Latham, Barbara, eds. *Chetham's Hospital School apprenticeships part 2, 1848-1945.* Fiche. Lancashire Family History & Heraldry Society, 2001

Leicestershire

Leicester

Hartopp, Henry, ed. *Register of the freemen of Leicester.* 2 pts. Records of the Borough of Leicester, new series, 1-2. 1927-33. Pt.1. 1196-1770, including the apprentices sworn before successive mayors for certain periods, 1646-1770. Pt.2. 1770-1930, including the apprentices sworn before successive mayors, 1770-1926.

Lincolnshire

Sturtivant, Doreen, & Sturtivant, Ray. *Lincolnshire masters & apprentices: Lincolnshire entries extracted from ledgers in the National Archives at Kew vols.1 & 2 - Town series IR 1/1 to IR 1/40 (1710-1810), Country series IR 1/41 to IR 1/7.* Lincolnshire Family History Society, 2007.

Sturtivant, Doreen, & Sturtivant, Ray. *Lincolnshire masters & apprentices: Lincolnshire entries from ledgers in the Public Record Office at Kew, vol.2: country series IR.1/41 to IR.1/72 (1711-1808).* Fiche. Lincolnshire Family History Society, 2003.

Cole, Anne E., et al. *An index to pauper apprenticeship indentures from 116 Lincolnshire parishes. Lincolnshire poor law index 5.* Lincolnshire Family History Society, 1991. For 1618-1857.

Boston

Westland, Richard A. *Apprentices & masters of Boston, Lincolnshire 1545-1717 as recorded in the assembly minutes of the corporation of Boston.* Fiche. Lincolnshire Family History Society, 1991

Pomeroy, Pat, ed. *Registers of apprentices at Boston Borough Council 1663-1903.* Fiche. Lincolnshire Family History Society, 1999.

Grimsby

Boswell, David. *Sea fishing apprentices of Grimsby.* Grimsby Public Libraries and Museum, 1973. Includes list of *'Casualties to Grimsby fishing apprentices: loss of life'.*

Horn, Pamela. 'Youth migration: the fisher boy apprentices of Grimsby, 1870-1914', *Genealogists' Magazine* 25(3), 1995, p.99-105.

Lunde, Karina, et al, eds. *Sea going apprentices of Grimsby, part 1: index of registers of sea fishing apprentices 1880-1937; part 2 index of sea fishing & merchant apprentices, 1879-1919 from other sources.* Humberside County Archive Service, 1990.

Wilson, John, ed. *Sea going apprentices of Grimsby: index 1879 to 1937.* South Humberside Area Archive Office, 1992.

Lincoln

Cole, Anne, & Mackinder, A. *Lincoln city apprentices registers, volume 1 (L1/5/2).* Fiche. Lincolnshire Family History Society, 1990. Covers 1640-1765.

Cole, Anne, & Mackinder, A. *Index to the Lincoln city apprentices registers.* 2 fiche. Lincolnshire Family History Society, 1992. Covers 1765-1867.

London & Middlesex

For a general history of London livery companies, see:

Unwin, George. *The gilds and companies of London.* 4th ed. Frank Cass & Co., 1963.

Many works relating to guilds, and including information about apprentices and freemen, are listed in:

Raymond, Stuart A. *Londoner's Occupations: a genealogical guide.* 2nd ed. Federation of Family History Societies, 2001.

The archives of city livery companies include much information on apprenticeship. See:

City livery companies and related organisations: a guide to their archives in Guildhall Library. 3rd ed. Guildhall Library, 1989.

An overview is offered by:

• *Searching for Members or those Apprenticed to Members of City of London* Livery Companies
  www.cityoflondon.gov.uk/Corporation/LGNL_Services/Leisure_and_cultur e/Records_and_archives/Visitor_information/free_information_leaflets.htm (click 'title').

See also:

• Sources for tracing apprenticeship and membership in City Livery Companies and related organisations
  www.history.ac.uk/gh/livdet.html

For medieval apprenticeship, see:

'Introduction: Apprenticeship', in Thomas, Arthur Hermann, ed. *Calendar of the plea and memoranda rolls of the city of London: volume 2: 1364-1381.* 1929, p. XXX-XLVII. **www.british-history.ac.uk/report.aspx?compid=36671**

Sources for freemen (including apprenticeship records) are discussed in:
Aldous, Vivienne E. *My ancestors were freemen of the City of London.* Society of Genealogists, 1999.

Freemen are listed, not very accurately, in:

Welch, Charles, ed. Register of the freemen of the City of London in the reigns of Henry VIII and Edward VI. London & Middlesex Archaeological Society, 1908. On this volume, see Marsh, Bower. 'A London manuscript', *Genealogist* New Series 32, 1916, p.217-20.

Freemen of 22 London companies are listed in:

Whitebrook, John Cudworth, ed. *London citizens in 1651, being a transcript of Harleian ms. 1778.* Hutchins & Romer, 1910.

Cliff Webb has compiled a series of indexes to livery company apprenticeship registers:

Webb, Clifford Reginald. *London livery company apprenticeship registers: abstracts and indexes.* Society of Genealogists, 1996- . Volumes include: 1. *Brewers 1685-1800.* 2. *Tylers and Bricklayers 1612-1644, 1668-1800.* 3. *Bowyers 1680-1806; Fletchers 1739-54; Longbowstringmakers 1604-68.* 4. *Glovers 1675-79, 1735-48, 1766-1804.* 5. *Glass-Sellers 1664-1812, Woolmen 1665-1828.* 6. *Broderers 1679-1713, 1763-1800. Combmakers 1744-50, Fanmakers 1775-1805, Framework Knitters 1727-30, Fruiterers 1750-1815, Gardeners 1764-1850, Horners 1731-1800.* 7. *Glaziers 1694-1800.* 8. *Gunmakers 1656-1800.* 9. *Needlemakers 1664-1801, Pinmakers 1691-1723.* 10. *Basketmakers 1639-1824.* 11. *Distillers 1659-1811.* 12. *Playing Card makers 1675-1760, Musicians 1765-1800, Saddlers 1657-1666, 1800 Tobacco pipemakers 1800.* 13. *Pattenmakers 1673-1805.* 14. *Spectaclemakers 1666-1800, Loriners 1722-31, 1759-1800.* 15. *Gold and Silver Wyre Drawers 1693-1837.* 16. *Tinplateworkers 1666, 1668, 1676, 1681, 1683-1800.* 17. *Innholders 1642-1643, 1654-1670, 1673-1800.* 18. *Poulters 1691-1729, 1754-1800.* 19. *Upholders 1704-1772.* 20. *Paviors 1568-1800.* 21. *Founders 1643-1800.* 22. *Armourers & Brasiers c1610-1800.* 23. *Coachmakers 1677-1800.* 24. *Ironmongers 1655-1800.* 25. *Dyers 1706-1746.* 26. *Cooks 1654-1800.* 27. *Masons 1663-1805.* 28. *Farriers 1619-1800.* 29. *Carmen 1668, 1678-1800.* 30. *Curriers 1628-1800.* 31. *Wax Chandlers 1666-1800; Brown Bakers 1615-1646.* 32. *Apothecaries 1617-69.* 33. *Plumbers 1571-1800.* 34. *Plasterers 1597-1662, 1698-1800.* 35. *Cutlers 1442-1448, 1565-1800.* 36. *Brewers 1531-1685.* 37. *Feltmakers 1676-1682, 1692-1800.* 38. *Painters and Stainers 1655, 1666-1800.* 39. *Tallow Chandlers 1633-1800.* 40. *Pewterers 1611-1900.* 41. *Blacksmiths 1605-1800.* 42. *Society of Apothecaries, 1670-1800, with Masons' Company 1619-1639.* 43. *Vintners 1609-1800.* 44. *Fishmongers 1614-1800.* 44-47. Not yet published. 48. *Grocers' Company 1629-1800.*

These registers, together with a number of others, are abstracted in:

• London Apprenticeship Abstracts 1442-1850.
  www.londonorigins.com/help/popup-aboutbo-lonapps.htm

See also:

Webb, Cliff. 'City of London apprenticeship and livery company records', *Genealogists magazine* 26(1), 1998, p.1-4.

Webb, Cliff. 'London apprenticeship records: a publication progress report', *Genealogists magazine* 28(3), 2004, p.104-6.

Armourers

'Apprentices and freemen of the Armourers Guild [London] from 1416 to the end of the reign of Edward VI [1553]', *Genealogists magazine* 9, 1940-46, p.179-92 & 217-22.

Book Trades

McKenzie, Donald Francis. 'Apprenticeship in the Stationers' Company, 1555-1640.' *The Library*, 5th series, 13, 1958, p.292-9.

McKenzie, Donald Francis. *Stationers' Company apprentices, 1605-40.* Charlottesville: Bibliographical Society of the University of Virginia, 1961.

McKenzie, Donald Francis, ed. *Stationers' Company apprentices, 1641-1700.* Oxford Bibliographical Society publications, New Series, 17. 1974

McKenzie, Donald Francis, ed. *Stationers' Company apprentices, 1701-1800.* Oxford Bibliographical Society publications, New Series, 19. 1978.

Arber, Edward ed. *A transcript of the registers of the Company of Stationers of London 1554-1640.* 5 vol. in 6 parts. 1875-94. Includes register of apprentices.

McKenzie, Donald Francis. 'A list of printers' apprentices 1605-40', *Studies in bibliography* 13, 1960, p.109-41.

Carpenters

Marsh, Bower, et al, eds. *Records of the Worshipful Company of Carpenters.* 7 vols. Oxford University Press, for the Company, 1913-68. Contents include v.1. Apprentices entry book, 1654-1694.

Clockmakers

Atkins, Charles Edward. *Register of apprenticeships of the Worshipful Company of Clockmakers of the City of London, from its incorporation in 1631 to its tercentenary in 1931 ...* Privately printed, 1931.

Drapers

Boyd, Percival. *Roll of the Drapers' Company of London: collected from the company's records and other sources.* J.A. Gordon, at the Andress Press, 1934.

Fishmongers

Haskett-Smith, Walter Parry. *The Worshipful Company of Fishmongers of the City of London: lists of apprentices and freemen in 1537 and 1600-50.* Privately published, 1916.

Mariners

Honourable Company of Master Mariners list of liverymen, members, apprentices & roll of retired members 1986-88. 3 vols. The Honourable Company of Master Mariners, 1986-88.

Shipwrights

Ridge, Cecil Harold, ed. *Records of the Worshipful Company of Shipwrights ... being an alphabetical digest of freemen and apprentices, etc.* 2 vols. Phillimore, 1939-46. Vol.1. 1428-1780. Vol.2. 1728-1858.

Skinners

Cokayne, George Edward, ed. 'Skinners Company: apprenticeships', *Miscellanea genealogica et heraldica* 3rd series 1, 1896, p.41-6, 76-80, 102-5, 149-52, 172-6, 194-6 & 246-53. Extracts, 1496-1515 and 1547-1694. Far from complete.

Watermen & Lightermen

Cottrell, Robert J. *Surname index to the Company of Watermen and Lightermen, London.* 9 folders + fiche. R.J.Cottrell, [1991]-6. Apprenticeship bindings, 1692-1949.

Weavers

Waller, William Chapman, ed. *Extracts from the court books of the Weavers Company of London, 1610-1730.* Publications of the Huguenot Society of London 33. 1931. Includes extensive information on apprentices.

Harrow

Golland, Jim. *The Harrow apprentices (1648-1871): a list of Harrow inhabitants whose apprenticeship fees were paid either by the governors of Harrow School, 1648-1871, or by the parish of Harrow, 1705-1803.* Harrow Public Libraries, 1981.

Threadneedle Street

Le May, Keith. 'The Threadneedle Street Church's Charity Schools: apprenticeships of former pupils', *Proceedings of the Huguenot Society of Great Britain & Ireland* 28(5), 2007, p.695-708. List, 18th c.

Westminster

Le May, Keith. 'The Westminster French Protestant Charity School: apprenticeships of former pupils', *Proceedings of the Huguenot Society of Great Britain & Ireland*, 27(4), 2001, p.561-72. List, late 18th c.

Norfolk

Great Yarmouth
Rutledge, Paul. *A calendar of Great Yarmouth enrolled apprenticeship indentures, 1563-1665.* Norfolk & Norwich Genealogical Society, [1979?]

Norwich
Rising, Winifred M., & Millican, Percy, eds. *An index of indentures of Norwich apprentices enrolled with the Norwich Assembly, Henry VII-George II.* Norfolk Record Society 29. 1959.

Millican, Percy, ed. *The register of the freemen of Norwich, 1548-1713: A transcript. With an introduction, an appendix to those freemen whose apprenticeship indentures are enrolled in the City Records, and indexes of names and places.* Norwich, 1934.

Millican, Percy, ed. *The freemen of Norwich, 1714-1752: a transcript of the third register.* Norfolk Record Society 23. 1952.

Northumberland

Newcastle upon Tyne
Dodds, Madelaine Hope, ed. *The register of freemen of Newcastle upon Tyne, from the corporation, guild and admission books chiefly of the seventeenth century.* Newcastle upon Tyne Records Committee publication 3. 1923.

Blair, Lesley Hunter, ed. *The register of freemen of Newcastle upon Tyne, from the corporation guild and admission books, chiefly of the eighteenth century.* Newcastle-upon-Tyne Records Committee publication 6. 1926.

Hostmen
Dendy, Frederick Walter, ed. *Extracts from the records of the Company of Hostmen of Newcastle-upon-Tyne.* Surtees Society, 105. 1901. Includes enrolments of apprentices, 1603-1874, and admissions of members, 1600-1901.

Merchant Adventurers
Dendy, Frederick Walter, ed. *Extracts from the records of the Merchant Adventurers of Newcastle-upon-Tyne.* 2 vols. Surtees Society 93 & 101. 1894-99. Includes enrolments of apprentices and freemen.

Saddlers

Hodgson, John. 'The Company of Saddlers of Newcastle', *Archaeologia Aeliana*, 3rd series 19, 1922, p.1-34. Includes a list of apprentices, 1590-1899.

Shipwrights

Rowe, David John, ed. *The records of the Company of Shipwrights of Newcastle-upon-Tyne, 1622-1967.* 2 vols. Surtees Society, 181 & 184. 1970-71. Vol.2 includes a list of members of the Company, including details of apprenticeship.

Nottinghamshire

Colwick

Bailey, Bryan, ed. *Colwick apprenticeship indentures 1800-10.* Records series, 123; Miscellany 13. Nottinghamshire Family History Society, 1999.

Cuckney

Apprentices at Toplis' mill, Cuckney 1786-1805. Records series 122. Nottinghamshire Family History Society, 1999.

Mansfield

A complete index of apprentices in Mansfield. Mansfield & District Family History Society, 1994. For 1720-1848; includes a register of parish apprentices, anno 1720, from the church of St. Peter & St. Paul, Mansfield.

Mansfield Woodhouse

Bailey, Bryan, ed. *Mansfield Woodhouse apprenticeship indentures 1738-91.* Records series 123. Miscellany 13. Nottinghamshire Family History Society, 1999.

Oxfordshire

Banbury

Gibson, Jeremy Sumner Wycherley. 'Some apprentices from eighteenth century Banbury', *Cake & cockhorse* 11(1), 1988, p.22-4.

Webb, Clifford Reginald. 'City of London Livery Companies: Apprentices from Banburyshire, sixteenth to eighteenth centuries', *Cake and Cockhorse*, 16(9), 2006, p.283-96.

Islip

Dr South's Charity School, Islip: vol. 1 apprentices 1717-1900, vol. 2 admissions & discharges 1800-1888. Eureka Partnership, 2003.

Oxford

Graham, Malcolm, ed. *Oxford City apprentices, 1697-1800*. Oxford Historical Society new series 31. 1987.

Staffordshire

- Staffordshire Apprenticeship Records
  www.staffsnameindexes.org.uk

Suffolk

Bury St. Edmunds
Plumridge, Peter. *Bury St. Edmunds workhouse & the poor of the town: apprenticeships, with lists of apprentices, masters & trades 1748-1830*. Bury St. Edmunds, 1998

Sudbury
Berry, Allan W. *Borough of Sudbury in Suffolk: inrollment of apprentices 1717-66*. Allan W. Berry, 1993.

Surrey

Jenkinson, Hilary, ed. *Surrey apprenticeships from the registers in the Public Record Office, 1711-1731*. Surrey Record Society 10. 1921. Also described as part 30 of the Society's publications.

Webb, Clifford Reginald, ed. *An index to Surrey apprenticeships, volume II, 1731-1749*. (being a continuation of Surrey Record Society volume X, 1929). Record series 6. West Surrey Family History Society, 1985.

The two works cited above are re-published in:

Surrey apprenticeships, 1711-1749. 3 fiche in folder. Microfiche series 12. West Surrey Family History Society, 1996.

Webb, Clifford Reginald, ed. *Surrey apprenticeships III: being an index of apprenticeships of Surrey interest from some London livery company records, 1563-1928*. Record series 33. West Surrey Family History Society, 2000.

Battersea
O'Sullivan, Maureen. *Battersea, Surrey: Index to apprenticeship records, 1602-1902*. Fiche. East Surrey Family History Society, 1988.

Camberwell

St. Giles, Camberwell: register of apprentices, 1802-17. Record publications 22. East Surrey Family History Society, 1987.

Croydon

Shaw, Herbert, & O'Sullivan, Maureen, eds. *Croydon, Surrey: index to apprenticeship registers, 1802-43; census, 1811.* Fiche. Record publications 3. East Surrey Family History Society, 1987.

Guildford

Carter, Hector, ed. *Guildford freemen's books, 1655-1933.* Guildford Corporation, 1963.

Kingston upon Thames

Daly, Anne, ed. *Kingston upon Thames register of apprentices, 1563-1713.* Surrey Record Society 28. 1974.

Mitcham

Mitcham, Surrey: indexes to settlement certificates, 1700-1806 (SRO LA5/5); bastardy examinations, 1715-1819 (LA5/7); apprenticeship indentures, 1700-1844 (LA5/6); apprenticeship registers, 1802-44 (P40/3/2 and 3); militia records, 1709-1811 (LA5/8). 2 fiche. Record publication 2. East Surrey Family History Society, 1987.

Mortlake

O'Sullivan, Maureen, ed. *Mortlake, Surrey: indexes to apprenticeship records, 1614-1915; (S.R.O. ref 2414/6); poor law records 1631-1834 (S.R.O. ref 2412/6); militia records 1801-1809 (S.R.O. ref 2414/8/24-26).* 2 fiche. Record publications 11. East Surrey Family History Society, 1987.

Reigate

O'Sullivan, Maureen, ed. *Reigate, Surrey: indexes to apprenticeship records 1672-1796 (S.R.O. ref P49/9); poor law records 1669-1794 (S.R.O. ref P49/4).* 2 fiche. Record publication 9. East Surrey Family History Society, 1987.

Wimbledon

O'Sullivan, Maureen, ed. *Wimbledon, Surrey: indexes to apprenticeship indentures, 1690-1895 (S.R.O. ref P5/5/962-969); poor law records 1698-1842 (S.R.O. ref P5/5, P5/14, & P5/17).* 2 fiche. Record publication 10. East Surrey Family History Society, 1987.

Sussex

Rice, Robert Garraway, ed. *Sussex apprentices and masters, 1710 to 1752, extracted from the apprenticeship books.* Sussex Record Society 28. 1924.

Warwickshire

Smith, Kelvin John, ed. *Warwickshire apprentices and their masters, 1710-1760.* Publications of the Dugdale Society 29. 1975. Abstracts from the Stamp Duty registers.

Morgan, Paul. *Warwickshire apprentices in the Stationers Company of London, 1563-1700.* Dugdale Society occasional papers 25. 1978. Includes 205 brief biographies.

Coventry
Robinson, Barbara, ed. *Coventry apprentice enrolment registers,* vol. 1-5: 1781-1841. Fiche. Coventry Family History Society, 1997-98.

Lane, Joan, ed. *Coventry apprentices and their masters, 1781-1806.* Publications of the Dugdale Society 33. 1983.

Wiltshire

Dale, Christabel, ed. *Wiltshire apprentices and their masters, 1710-1760.* Wiltshire Archaeological and Natural History Society Records Branch 17. 1961.

Henly, H.R., ed. *The apprentice registers of the Wiltshire Society, 1817-1922.* Wiltshire Record Society 51. 1997.

Henly, H.R. 'The Wiltshire Feast', *Genealogists Magazine* 24(9), 1994, p.393-8.

Broad Town
Carter, Barbara J. *Broad Town charity apprentices [1711-1909].* Fiche. Wiltshire Family History Society, 1996.

Salisbury
Hurley, Beryl, ed. *Salisbury area apprenticeships [1688-1902] & Wilton Free School [registers 1723-1907].* Wiltshire Family History Society, 1996.

Yorkshire

Keighley
Isaac Bowcock's Charity: index of apprenticeships indentures 1834-1913. Keighley Family History Publishing, 1997. A Keighley charity.

Sheffield
Leader, Robert Eadon. *History of the Company of Cutlers in Hallamshire, in the county of York.* 2 vols. Pawson & Brailsford, 1905-6. Vol.2 lists over 28,500 apprentices and freemen. This information is also available on a database:

- Sheffield Records Online: Sheffield Master Cutlers and Apprentices **www.sheffieldrecordsonline.org.uk/index_cutlers.html**

York
Malden, John. 'Freemen & apprentices of York', in *English genealogical congress: selected papers given at the congresses of 1978 & 1984.* English Genealogical Congress, 1986

Collins, Frederick, ed. *Register of the freemen of the City of York, from the city records.* 2 vols. Surtees Society 96 & 102. v.1. 1272-1558. v.2. 1559-1759.

Malden, John, ed. *Register of York Freemen 1680-1986.* William Sessions Ltd., 1989. Includes apprenticeships, 1573-1688 & 1727-1862.

Bisset, Anna B. *The Eastland Company York Residence: register of admissions to the Company, 1646-1689, and register of apprentices 1642-1696.* Borthwick list and index 17. York: University of York, 1996.

Cotterell, Howard Herschel. *York pewterers, being a list of all those pewterers who were freemen of the City of York, or of the pewterers' Guild of York, or were apprenticed to freemen, covering the period 1272-1835.* John Bellows, 1916.

Scotland

Watson, Charles Brodie Boog, ed. *The register of apprentices of the City of Edinburgh 1583-1666.* Scottish Record Society [old series], 28, 1906.

Watson, Charles Brodie Boog, ed. *Register of Edinburgh apprentices 1666-1700.* Scottish Record Society [old series] 60. 1929.

Watson, Charles Brodie Boog, ed. *Register of Edinburgh apprentices 1701-55.* Scottish Record Society [old series] 61. 1929.

Wood, Marguerite, ed. *The register of Edinburgh apprentices 1756-1800. Scottish Record Society* [old series] 92. 1963.

NOTES

1. Thomas, A. H., ed. *Calendar of the plea and memoranda rolls of the city of London: volume 2: 1364-1381*. 1929. **www.british-history.ac.uk/source.aspx?pubid=162**
2. Dilks, Thomas Bruce, ed. *Bridgwater borough archives 1400-1445*. Somerset Record Society 58. 1945, p.80.
3. Ricart, Robert. *The maire of Bristowe is kalendar*, ed. Lucy Toulmin Smith. Camden Society new series 5. 1872, p.102.
4. Thrupp, Sylvia. *The merchant class of medieval London [1306-1500]*. University of Chicago Press, 1968, pp.215-6.
5. These are listed at Archon **www.nationalarchives.gov.uk/archon**.
6. Rappaport, Steve. *Worlds within worlds: structures of life in sixteenth-century London*. Cambridge University Press, 1989, p.232.
7. Barlow, Jill, ed. *A Calendar of the registers of the apprentices of the City of Gloucester, 1595-1700*. Gloucestershire record series 14. Bristol & Gloucestershire Archaeological Society, 2001, p.xxiii-xxiv.
8. In a few places, such as Walsham le Willows, Essex, and Colyton, Devon, apprentices had been bound out by the parish before these acts were passed. See Hindle, Steve. 'Waste children: pauper apprenticeship under the Elizabethan poor laws, c.1598-1697', in Lane, Penelope, Raven, Neil, & Snell, K.D.M., eds. *Women, work and wages in England 1600-1850*. Boydell Press, 2004, p.27.
9. Ibid, p.35. This figure is calculated from Privy Council returns of 1634-6. In the eighteenth-century East Midlands and East Anglia, a third of parish apprentices were female; cf. Hill, Bridget. *Women, work & sexual politics in eighteenth-century England*. UCE Press, 1994, p.86.
10. Lane, Joan. *Apprenticeship in England, 1600-1914*. UCL Press, 1996, p.1.
11. Lane, Joan. 'Apprenticeship in Warwickshire cotton mills, 1790-1830', *Textile history* 10, 1979, p.162.
12. Lane, Joan. *Apprenticeship in England, 1600-1914*. UCL Press, 1996, p.230.

13. Brooks, Christopher. 'Apprenticeship, social mobility, and the middling sort, 1550-1800', in Barry, Jonathan, & Brooks, Christopher, eds. *The middling sort of people: culture, society and politics in England, 1550-1800*. Macmillan, 1994, pp.52-83.

14. p.33

15. Graham, Malcolm, ed. *Oxford City apprentices, 1697-1800*. Oxford Historical Society new series 31. 1987, p.xxiii.

16. I owe this information to Cliff Webb.

17. Unwin, Joan. 'Apprenticeships and freedoms: the computer analysis of the records of the Cutlers Company', *Local historian* 25(4), 1995, p.204.

18. Jenkinson, Hilary, ed. *Surrey apprenticeships from the registers in the Public Record Office, 1711-1731*. Surrey Record Society 10. 1921. Also described as no. 30 of the Society's publications.

19. Graham, Malcolm, ed. *Oxford City apprentices, 1697-1800*. Oxford Historical Society new series 31. 1987, p.xiv.

20. Willis, Arthur J., & Merson, A. L., eds. *A calendar of Southampton apprenticeship registers, 1609-1740*. Southampton Records series, 12. 1968, p.xxxiv.

21. I owe this information to Cliff Webb.

22. Some examples of indentures are given below, pp.33-37.

23. Vanes, Jean. *Education and apprenticeship in sixteenth-century Bristol*. Historical Association Bristol Branch, 1982, p.3.

24. Willis & Merson, op cit, p.37.

25. Ibid, p.xxii.

26. Patten, John. 'Patterns of migration and movement of labour to three pre-industrial East Anglian towns', *Journal of historical geography* 2(2), 1976, p.126.

27. Steer, Francis W., ed. *Scriveners Company common paper 1357-1628*. London Record Society 4. 1968, pp.xi & 51-2.

28. Honeyman, Katrina. *Child workers in England, 1780-1820: parish apprentices and the making of the early industrial labour force*. Studies in labour history. Ashgate, 2007, pp.179-86.

29. Dunlop, O. J. *English apprenticeship and child labour: a history*. T. Fisher Unwin, 1912, pp.57-8.

30. Barlow, Jill, ed. *A calendar of the registers of apprentices of the City of Gloucester, 1595-1700*. Gloucestershire record series 14. 2001, p.129.

31. Ibid, p.237.

32. Rowe, D. J., ed. *The records of the Company of Shipwrights of Newcastle upon Tyne, 1622-1967*. Volume 1. Selden Society 81. 1970, p.43.

33. Graham, Malcolm, ed. *Oxford City apprentices, 1697-1800*. Oxford Historical Society new series 31. 1987, p.xxiii.

34. Barlow, Jill, ed. *A Calendar of the registers of the apprentices of the City of Gloucester, 1595-1700*. Gloucestershire record series 14. Bristol & Gloucestershire Archaeological Society, 2001, p.xx.

35. Ibid, p.222.

36. Graham, op cit, p.xxiii.

37. Rappaport, Steve. *Worlds within worlds: structures of life in sixteenth-century London*. Cambridge University Press, 1989, p.233.

38. Ben-Amos, Ilana Krausman. 'Failure to become freemen: urban apprentices in early modern England', *Social history* 16(2), 1991, p.155.

39. Levene, Alyson. 'Honesty, sobriety and diligence: master-apprentice relations in eighteenth-and nineteenth-century England', *Social history* 33(2), p.2008, p.190.

40. Ditto.

41. Barlow, op cit, p.xv.

42. Ben-Amos, op cit, p.169.

43. Brooks, Christopher. 'Apprenticeship, social mobility, and the middling sort, 1550-1800', in Barry, Jonathan, & Brooks, Christopher, eds. *The middling sort of people: culture, society and politics in England, 1550-1800*. Macmillan, 1994, p.63.

44. Dunlop, O. J. *English apprenticeship and child labour: a history*. T. Fisher Unwin, 1912, pp.53 & 200.

45. Graham, Malcolm, ed. *Oxford City apprentices, 1697-1800*. Oxford Historical Society new series 31. 1987, p.xx.

46. Dunlop, op cit, p.211; Lane, Joan. *Apprenticeship in England, 1600-1914*. UCL Press, 1996, p.199.

47. This has been worked out by Cliff Webb.

48. Butcher, E. E., ed. *Bristol Corporation of the Poor: selected records, 1696-1834*. Bristol Record Society 3. 1932, p.60.

49. Taylor, Royston, et al, eds. *Calendar of the court books of the Borough of New Woodstock, 1607-1622*. Oxfordshire Record Society 65. 2007, p.155.

50. Connor, W .J., ed. *The Southampton mayor's book of 1606-1608*. Southampton records series 21. 1978, p.52.

51. Willis, Arthur J., & Merson, A. L., eds. *A calendar of Southampton apprenticeship registers, 1609-1740*. Southampton Records series, 12. 1968, p.xxxiii & lxxvii; Graham, Malcolm, ed. *Oxford City apprentices, 1697-1800*. Oxford Historical Society new series 31. 1987, xxvii.

52. Barlow, Jill, ed. *A Calendar of the registers of the apprentices of the City of Gloucester 1595-1700*. Gloucestershire record series 14. Bristol & Gloucestershire Archaeological Society, 2001, p.xxvi.

53. Patten, John. 'Patterns of migration and movement of labour to three East Anglian towns', *Journal of historical geography* 2(2), 1976, p.114.

54. Woodward, D. M. 'Freemen's rolls', *Local historian* 9(2), 1970, p.92.

55. Barlow, Jill, ed. *A Calendar of the registers of the apprentices of the City of Gloucester, 1595-1700* . Gloucestershire record series 14. Bristol & Gloucestershire Archaeological Society, 2001.

56. Graham, Malcolm, ed. *Oxford City apprentices, 1697-1800*. Oxford Historical Society new series 31. 1987, p.xx.

57. More information on the movement of London apprentices will be found in forthcoming papers from Cliff Webb and Patrick Wallis.

58. Smith, Steven R. 'The social and geographical origins of the London apprentices', *Guildhall miscellany* 4(4), 1973, p.201.

59. Ibid, p.200.

60. Massinger, Philip. *The plays and poems of Philip Massinger*, ed. Philip Edwards & Colin Gibson. Clarendon Press, 1976, vol.4, p.92.

61. Smith, op cit, p.205.

62. Dunlop, O. J. *English apprenticeship and child labour: a history*. T.Fisher Unwin, 1912, p.107-33.

63. Quated by ibid, p.244.

64. Parr, Joy. *Labouring children: British immigrant apprentices to Canada 1869-1924*. Croom Helm, 1980.

65. Dunlop, O. J. *English apprenticeship and child labour: a history*. T.Fisher Unwin, 1912, p.76.

66. Hodgson, J. C. 'The Company of Saddlers of Newcastle', *Archaeologia Aeliana* 3rd series 19, 1922, p.9.

67. Rowe, D. J., ed. *The records of the Company of Shipwrights of Newcastle-upon-Tyne, 1622-1967. Volume 1*. Surtees Society 81. 1970, p.10.

68. Lane, Joan, ed. *Coventry apprentices and their masters, 1781-1806*. Publications of the Dugdale Society 33. 1983, p.xi.

69. Laurence, Anne. *Women in England 1500-1700*. St. Martins Press, 1994, p.126.

70. Ibid, p.127.

71. Rising, Winifred M., & Millican, Percy, eds. *An index of indentures of Norwich apprentices enrolled with the Norwich Assembly, Henry VII-George II*. Norfolk Record Society '29. 1959, p.xiii.

72. Hughes, T. Cann, ed. *The rolls of the freemen of the Borough of Lancaster, 1688 to 1840. Part 1*. Lancashire & Cheshire Record Society 87. 1935, p.v.

73. Barlow, Jill, ed., *A calendar of the register of apprentices of the City of Gloucester, 1595-1700*. Bristol & Gloucestershire Archaeological Society 14. 2001, p.xiv.

74. Rising, Winifred M., & Millican, Percy, eds. *An index of indentures of Norwich apprentices enrolled with the Norwich Assembly, Henry VII-George II*. Norfolk Record Society, 29. 1959, p.xii.

75. Dunlop, op cit, p.164.

76. The hostmen were merchants who controlled the coal trade in Newscastle.

77. Dendy, F.W., ed. *Extracts from the records of the Company of Hostmen of Newcastle-upon-Tyne.* Surtees Society 105. 1901, p.103.

78. Ibid, p.160.

79. Ibid, p.130.

80. Ibid, p.165.

81. Ibid, p.201.

82. Ibid, p.181.

83. Dendy, F. W., ed. *Extracts from the records of the Merchant Adventurers of Newcastle-upon-Tyne. Vol.2.* Surtees Society 101. 1899.

84. Matthews, Harold Evan, ed. *Proceedings, minutes and enrolments of the Company of Soapmakers, 1562-1642.* Bristol Record Society 10. 1940, p.25.

85. Dunlop, O. J. *English apprenticeship and child labour: a history.* T. Fisher Unwin, 1912, op cit, pp.216 & 218.

86. Kahl, William F. 'Apprenticeship and the freedom of the London livery companies, 1690-1750', *Guildhall miscellany* 1(7), 1952-9, p.17.

87. Reillo, Giorgio. 'The shaping of a family trade: the Cordwainers Company in eighteenth-century London', in Gadd, Ian Anders, & Wallis, Patrick, eds. *Guilds, society and economy in London, 1450-1800.* Centre for Metropolitan History, 2002, p.146.

88. Barlow, op cit, p.xv.

89. Brooks, Christopher. 'Apprenticeship, social mobility, and the middling sort, 1550-1800', in Barry, Jonathan, & Brooks, Christopher, eds. *The middling sort of people: culture, society and politics in England, 1550-1800.* Macmillan, 1994, p.65.

90. Millican, Percy, ed. *The freemen of Norwich, 1714-1752.* Norfolk Record Society 23. 1952, introduction (unpaginated).

91. Aldous, Vivienne E. *My ancestors were freemen of the City of London.* Society of Genealogists, 1999, p.13.

92. Dodds, Madelaine Hope, ed. *The register of freemen of Newcastle upon Tyne, from the Corporation, guild and admission books chiefly of the seventeenth century.* Newcastle upon Tyne records committee 3, 1923, p.ix-xi.

93. Dunlop, O. J. *English apprenticeship and child labour: a history.* T. Fisher Unwin, 1912, p.87

94. Ben-Amos, Ilana Krausman. 'Failure to become freemen: urban apprentices in early modern England', *Social history* 16(2), 1991, p.159.

95. Dunlop, O. J. *English apprenticeship and child labour: a history.* T. Fisher Unwin, 1912, p.53 & 69-70.

96. Connor, W. J., ed. *The Southampton mayor's book of 1606-1608.* Southampton records series 21. 1978, p.59.

97. Willis, Arthur J., & Merson, A. L., eds. *A calendar of Southampton apprenticeship registers, 1609-1740.* Southampton Records series 12. 1968, op cit, p.xxix.

98. Unwin, Joan. 'Apprenticeships and freedoms : the computer analysis of the records of the Cutlers' Company in Sheffield', *Local Historian* 25(4), 1995, pp.194-208.

99. Hughes, T. Cann, ed. *The rolls of the freemen of the Borough of Lancaster, 1688 to 1840*. Lancashire & Cheshire Record Society 87. 1935, p.vi-vii.

100. Dendy, F.W., ed. *Extracts from the records of the Company of Hostmen of Newcastle-upon-Tyne*. Surtees Society, 101. 1901, p.160.

101. Graham, Malcolm, ed. *Oxford City apprentices, 1697-1800*. Oxford Historical Society new series 31. 1987, p.83.

102. Child, Sarah. 'Parish apprentices in Rackenford, 1728-1844', *Devonshire Association ... Report & Transactions* 136, 2004, pp.135-48

103. Marshall,William. *The rural economy of the West of England ... Vol.1*. G.Nicol, 1796, p.10.

104. Cited by McClure, Ruth K. *Coram's children: the London Foundling Hospital in the eighteenth century*. Yale Universtiy Press, 1981, pp.117-8.

105. Honeyman, Katrina. *Child workers in England, 1780-1820: parish apprentices and the making of the early industrial labour force*. Studies in labour history. Ashgate, 2007, pp.216-7 & 238.

106. Butcher, E. E., ed. *Bristol Corporation of the Poor, 1696-1834*. Bristol Record Society 3. 1932, p.60.

107. Honeyman, op cit, p.25.

108. Honeyman, op cit, p.24.

109. Honeyman, op cit, pp.29-30.

110. Pugh, R. K., ed. *The letter book of Samuel Wilberforce, 1843-68*. Oxfordshire Record Society 47. 1970, p.5.

111. Quoted by 'Apprenticeship of Workhouse Children' **www.workhouses.org.uk/index.html?education/apprenticeship.htmls**

112. Ibid, p.127.

113. Hill, Bridget. *Women, work, & Sexual politics in eighteenth-century England*. UCL Press, 1994, p.102.

114. Gretton, Mary Sturge, ed. *Oxfordshire Justices of the Peace in the seventeenth century*. Oxfordshire Record Society 16. 1934, p.xxvi.

115. Lane, Joan, ed. *Coventry apprentices and their masters, 1781-1806*. Publications of the Dugdale Society 33. 1983, p.xi.

116. Horn, Pamela. 'The traffic in children and the textile mills, 1780-1816', *Genealogists Magazine* 24(5), 1993, p.178.

117. Honeyman, Katrina. *Child workers in England, 1780-1820: parish apprentices and the making of the early industrial labour force*. Studies in labour history. Ashgate, 2007, p.149.

118. Ibid, pp.125 & 126.

119. Lane, Joan. Apprenticeship in Warwickshire cotton mills, 1790-1830', *Textile history* 10, 1979, p.166.

120. Honeyman, Katrina. 'The parish apprentice and textile industries in the North', *Northern history* 44, 2007, p.117. Ditto, *Child workers in England ...*, pp.243 &259.

121. Honeyman, 'The parish apprentice', ..., pp.119-20.

122. Ibid, p.138.

123. Honeyman, Katrina. *Child workers in England, 1780-1820: parish apprentices and the making of the early industrial labour force.* Studies in labour history. Ashgate, 2007, p.149.

124. Crompton, Frank. *Workhouse children.* Sutton, 1997, pp.20-21.

125. Horn, Pamela. 'Pauper apprenticeship and the Grimsby fishing industry, 1870 to 1914', *Labour history review* 61(2), 1996, p.177.

126. Ditto.

127. Lane, Joan, ed. *Coventry apprentices and their masters,* 1781-1806. Publications of the Dugdale Society 33. 1983, p.xi.

128. Graham, Malcolm, ed. *Oxford City apprentices, 1697-1800.* Oxford Historical Society new series 31. 1987, p.xxi.

129. Willis, Arthur J., & Merson, A. L., eds. *A calendar of Southampton apprenticeship registers, 1609-1740.* Southampton Records series 12. 1968, p.lxvi-lxxiv.

130. Barlow, Jill, ed. *A Calendar of the registers of the apprentices of the City of Gloucester, 1595-1700.* Gloucestershire record series 14. Bristol & Gloucestershire Archaeological Society, 2001, p.xx & passim.

131. Robin, Jean. *The way we lived then.* Ashgate, 2000, p.133.

132. I owe this information to Cliff Webb.

133. Henly, H.R., ed. *The apprentice registers of the Wiltshire Society, 1817-1922.* Wiltshire Record Society 51. 1997.

134. Levene, Alysa. 'Honesty, sobriety and diligence: master-parent relations in eighteenth-and nineteenth-century England', *Social history* 33(2), 2008, p.183-200; Clark, Gillian. 'Records of Thomas Coram's Foundling Hospital', *Genealogists Magazine* 27(5), 2002, p.214-9. Its records are described online in 'Finding your Foundling' **www.cityoflondon.gov.uk/Corporation/LGNL_Services/Leisure_and_culture/ Records_and_archives/Visitor_information/free_information_leaflets.htm** (click 'Foundling Hospital').

135. Lemay, Keith. 'The Westminster French Protestant Charity School: apprenticeships of former pupils, 1750-1815', *Proceedings of the Huguenot Society of Great Britain & Ireland* 27(4), 2001, pp.561-72.

136. Smail, John, ed. *Woollen manufacturing in Yorkshire: the memorandum book of John Brearley, cloth frizzer at Wakefield, 1758-1762.* Yorkshire Archaeological Society Record Series 155. 2001, p.47.

137. Barlow, Jill, ed. *A Calendar of the registers of the apprentices of the City of Gloucester, 1595-1700.* Gloucestershire record series 14. Bristol & Gloucestershire Archaeological Society, 2001, pp.xx-xxii.

138. Youings, Joyce. *Tuckers' Hall, Exeter: the history of a provincial city company through five centuries.* University of Exeter, 1968, p.138-9.

139. Devon Record Office. ECM58/7/9/3/1-12.

140. Henly, H. R., ed. *The apprentice registers of the Wiltshire Society, 1817-1922.* Wiltshire Record Society 51. 1997.

141. Willis, Arthur J., & Merson, A. L., eds. *A calendar of Southampton apprenticeship registers, 1609-1740.* Southampton Records series 12. 1968, p.95.

142. Barlow, Jill, ed. *A Calendar of the registers of the apprentices of the City of Gloucester, 1595-1700.* Gloucestershire record series 14. Bristol & Gloucestershire Archaeological Society, 2001, p.xxiii.

143. These are listed at Archon **www.nationalarchives.gov.uk/archon**.

144. For a listing of useful sites, see Raymond, Stuart *A. Family history on the web: an internet directory for England & Wales*. 5th ed. Family History Partnership, 2008.

145. Add. mss. 26882.

146. These are listed at **www.ffhs.org.uk/members2/contacting.php**.

147. For help with these problems, a number of tutorials are available at **www.nationalarchives.gov.uk/records/reading-old-documents.htm**

148. Smith, K. J., ed. *Warwickshire apprentices and their masters 1710-1760*. Publications of the Dugdale Society 29.1975, p.x.

149. Churchill, Else. 'Munimenta antiqua and Crisp's and Clench's collections of original apprenticeship indentures 1641-1888, and original marriage licences', *Genealogists' Magazine* 28(3), 2004, pp.101-3.

150. Devon Record Office ECA Apprenticeship Indentures, series 2, no.1.

151. Rowe, Margery M., & Jackson, Andrew M., eds. *Exeter freemen, 1266-1967*. Devon & Cornwall Record Society extra series 1. 1973, passim.

152. 'seven' deleted, 'eight' interlined.

153. 'next ensueing' interlined.

154. Deleted in mss.

155. Devon Record Office, ECA/Book 227A.

156. Devon Record Office 3004A/PO193/3/1

157. For borough court records, see below, p.60

158. Barlow, Jill, ed. *A Calendar of the registers of the apprentices of the City of Gloucester, 1595-1700*. Gloucestershire record series 14. Bristol & Gloucestershire Archaeological Society, 2001, p.xiv.

159. A number of borough apprenticeship registers have been published, and are listed under 'published sources' below, pp.83-101

160. Maslen, Marjorie, ed. *Woodstock chamberlains' accounts*, 1609-50. Oxfordshire Record Society 58. 1993, p.191.

161. Willis, Arthur J., & Merson, A.L., eds. *A calendar of Southampton apprenticeship registers, 1609-1740*. Southampton Records series, 12. 1968, p.lxx.

162. Daly, Anne, ed. *Kingston upon Thames register of apprentices, 1563-1713*. Surrey Record Society 28. 1974, p.xi.

163. Lane, Joan, ed. *Coventry apprentices and their masters, 1781-1806*. Publications of the Dugdale Society 33. 1983, passim.

164. For bibliographical details, see below, pp.83-101

165. Blair, Lesley Hunter, ed. *The register of freemen of Newcastle upon Tyne, from the corporation guild and admission books, chiefly of the eighteenth century*. Newcastle-upon-Tyne Records Committee Publications 6. 1926, p.xi.

166. Dodds, Madelaine Hope, ed. *The register of freemen of Newcastle upon Tyne, from the Corporation, guild and admission books chiefly of the seventeenth century*. Newcastle upon Tyne records committee 3, 1923, p.ix.

167. Devon Record Office ECA 227.

168. Youings, Joyce. *Tuckers Hall, Exeter: the history of a provincial city company through five centuries*. University of Exeter, 1968, p.235.

169. Unwin, George. *The gilds and companies of London*. 4th ed. Frank Cass & Co., 1963.

170. See the guide, 'Searching for Members or those apprenticed to Members of City of London Livery Companies' **www.cityoflondon.gov.uk/Corporation/LGNL_Services/ Leisure_and_culture/Records_and_archives/Visitor_information/free_ information_leaflets.htm**. These records were formerly in Guildhall Library, and are described in detail in *City livery companies and related organisations: a guide to their archives in Guildhall Library*. 3rd ed. Guildhall Library, 1989. See also the list in Rappaport, Steve. *Worlds within worlds: structures of life in sixteenth-century London*. Cambridge University Press, 1989, pp.408-16.

171. Listed below, p.92

172. London Apprenticeship Abstracts 1442-1850
www.londonorigins.com/help/popup-aboutbo-lonapps.htm

173. See Aldous, Vivienne E. *My ancestors were freemen of the City of London*. Society of Genealogists, 1999.

174. Matthews, Harold Evans, ed. *Proceedings, minutes and enrolments of the Company of Soapmakers, 1562-1642*. Bristol Record Society 10. 1940, p.121.

175. Willis, Arthur J., & Merson, A. L., eds. *A calendar of Southampton apprenticeship registers, 1609-1740*. Southampton Records series, 12. 1968, pp.61-108.

176. Devon Record Office 3483 A/PO 24.

177. See below, p.87

178. Gibson, Jeremy, et al. *Poor Law Union records*. 4 vols. 2nd/3rd ed. 1997-2008.

179. Thompson, Kathryn. 'Apprenticeship and the new poor law: a Leicestershire example', *Local historian* 19(2), 1989, p.51.

180. Levene, Alysa. 'Honesty, sobriety, and diligence: master-apprentice relations in eighteenth- and nineteenth-century England', *Social history* 33(2), 2008, pp.183-200.

181. For a detailed discussion, visit 'Apprenticeship Records as Sources for Genealogy' **www.nationalarchives.gov.uk/catalogue/RdLeaflet.asp?sLeafletID=295** .

182. This has been worked out by Cliff Webb.

183. For these, see below, pp.89-99

184. 'Cambridgeshire Masters and their Apprentices 1763-1811'
www.cfhs.org.uk/Apprentices/index.html

185. This database is currently (2010) being re-keyed for better search functionality. It may be moved to another website in 2011. Visit **www.sog.org.uk** for news on its future.

186. For churchwardens' accounts, see Cox, J.Charles. *Churchwardens accounts from the fourteenth century to the close of the seventeenth century*. Methuen, 1913.

187. Botelho, L. A., ed. *Churchwardens accounts of Cratfield, 1640-1660*. Suffolk Records Society 42. 1999, p.86 & 107.

188. Hassall, W. O., ed. *Wheatley records, 956-1956*. Oxfordshire Record Society 37. 1956, p.67.

189. Honeyman, Katrina. *Child workers in England, 1780-1820: parish apprentices and the making of the early industrial labour force*. Studies in labour history. Ashgate, 2007, pp.29-30.

190. Anderson, Philip. *The Leeds Workhouse under the old poor law, 1728-1834*. Publications of the Thoresby Soceity 56. 1981, p.112.

191. Lane, Joan. *Apprenticeship in England, 1600-1914*. UCL Press, 1996, p.86.

192. Hutton, Ronald. *The rise and fall of merry England: the ritual year 1400-1700*. Oxford Univeristy Press, 1994, p.263-93.

193. Hitchcock, Tim, & Black, John, eds. *Chelsea settlement and bastardy examinations, 1733-1766*. London Record Society 33. 1999, p.79

194. Gray, Irvine, ed. *Cheltenham settlement examinations, 1815-1826*. Bristol & Gloucestershire Archaeological Society Records Section 7. 1969, p.39.

195. Johnson, H. C., ed. *Wiltshire county records: minutes of proceedings in sessions 1563 and 1574 to 1592*. Wiltshire Record Society 4. 1948, p.52.

196. Cockburn, J. S., ed. *Somerset assize orders, 1640-1659*. Somerset Record Society 71. 1971, p.9.

197. Morgan, Gwenda, & Rushton, Peter, eds. *The justicing notebook (1750-64) of Edmund Tew, rector of Boldon*. Surtees Society 205. 2000, pp.41, 84 & 86.

198. Taylor, Royston, et al, eds. *Calendar of the court book of the Borough of New Woodstock, 1607-1622*. Oxfordshire Record Society 65. 2007, p.352.

199. Anderson, R.C., ed. *The book of examinations and depositions, 1622-1644. Vol. II. 1607-1634*. Southampton Record Society 31. 1931, pp.124-6.

200. Tarver, Anne. *Church court records: an introduction for family and local historians*. Phillimore, 1995.

201. Many London apprentices are indexed in Giese, Loreen, ed. *London Consistory Court depositions, 1686-1611: lists and indexes*. London Record Society 32. 1995.

202. Ratcliffe, Richard. *Basic facts about ... Quarter Session records*. Federation of Family History Societies, 2007.

203. Gibson, Jeremy. *Quarter sessions records for family historians: a select list*. 5th ed. Family History Partnership, 2008.

204. Darlington, Ida, ed. *London Consistory Court wills, 1492-1547*. London Record Society 3. 1967, p.76.

205. Hickman, David, ed. *Lincoln wills, 1532-1534*. Lincoln Record Society 89. 2001, p.308.

206. Willis, Arthur J., & Merson, A.L., eds. *A calendar of Southampton apprenticeship registers, 1609-1740*. Southampton Records series, 12. 1968, p.lxvii.

207. Gibson, Jeremy, & Churchill, Else. *Probate jurisdictions: where to look for wills*. 6th ed. Family History Partnership, forthcoming.

208. Grannum, Karen, & Taylor, Nigel. *Wills & probate records: a guide for family historians*. 2nd ed. National Archives, 2009.

209. Gibson, Jeremy, & Rogers, Colin. *Poll books 1696-1872: a directory to holdings in Great Britain*. 4th ed. Family History Partnership, 2008.

210. Lane, Joan. 'Apprenticeship in Warwickshire cotton mills, 1790-1830', *Textile history* 10, 1979, pp.161-74.

211. Dunlop, O.J. *English apprenticeship and child labour: a history*. T.Fisher Unwin, 1912, pp.360-2.

212. Cockton, P. *Subject catalogue of the House of Commons papers, 1801-1900.* 5 vols. Chadwyck-Healey, 1988. See also Bopcris: British Official Publications Collaborative Readers Guide **www.bopcris.ac.uk**

213. Bopcris: British Official Publications Collaborative Readers guide **www.bopcris.ac.uk**

214. Butcher, E. E., ed. *The Bristol Corporation of the Poor 1696-1834.* Bristol Record Society 3. 1931, p.120.

215. Ibid, p.122.

216. Cited by Lane, Joan, ed. *Coventry apprentices and their masters, 1781-1806.* Publications of the Dugdale Society 33. 1983, p.x.

217. Quoted by Douch, H. L. 'Gone away', *Journal of the Royal Institution of Cornwall*, new series II, 1(1), 1991, p.89.

218. Quoted by Douch, H. L. 'Gone away', *Journal of the Royal Institution of Cornwall*, new series II, 1(1), 1991, p.95.

219. British Newspapers 1800-1900 **http://newspapers.bl.uk/blcs**

220. Gibson, Jeremy, Langston, Brett, & Smith, Brenda W. *Local newspapers 1750-1920: England and Wales, Channel Islands, Isle of Man: a select location list.* 2nd ed. Federation of Family History Societies, 2002.

221. Abstracts are taken from either Darby Pickering's *Statutes at large ...* (1763-), or from *The statutes of the realm* (Record Commissioners, 1811). The wording given in these sources is not always identical, and I have modernised spellings. The titles of acts are also mine.

222. Dunlop, O. J. *English apprenticeship and child labour: a history.* T. Fisher Unwin, 1912, p.91.

223. Dunlop, O. J. *English apprenticeship and child labour: a history.* T. Fisher Unwin, 1912, p.74.

224. *Calendar of State Papers Domestic ... James I, 1603-1610.* 1857, p.342.

225. Willis, Arthur J., & Merson, A. L., eds. *A calendar of Southampton apprenticeship registers, 1609-1740.* Southampton Records series, 12. 1968, p.xi.

226. Quoted in Hindle, Steve. 'Waste children: pauper apprenticeship under the Elizabethan poor laws, c.1598-1697', in Lana, Penelope, Raven, Neil & Snell, K.D.M., eds. *Women, work, and wages in England, 1600-1850.* Boydell Press, 2004, p.22.

227. Hindle, Steve. 'Waste children: pauper apprenticeship under the Elizabethan poor laws, c.1598-1697', in Lane, Penelope, Raven, Neil, & Snell, K.D.M., eds. *Women, work and wages in England 1600-1850.* Boydell Press, 2004, p.23.

228. Rice, R. Garraway, ed. *Sussex apprentices and masters, 1710 to 1752, extracted from the apprenticeship books.* Sussex Record Society 28. 1924.

229. Quoted by Webb, Sidney, & Webb, Beatrice. *English poor law history, part II: the last hundred years.* Volume 1. 1929, p.295.

230. Webb, op cit, p.294.

About the SOCIETY
OF GENEALOGISTS

Founded in 1911 the Society of Genealogists (SoG) is Britain's premier family history organisation. The Society maintains a splendid genealogical library and education centre in Clerkenwell.

The Society's collections are particularly valuable for research before the start of civil registration of births marriages and deaths in 1837 but there is plenty for the beginner too. Anyone starting their family history can book free help sessions in the open community access area where assistance can be given in searching online census indexes or looking for entries in birth, death and marriage indexes.

The Library contains Britain's largest collection of parish register copies, indexes and transcripts and many nonconformist registers. Most cover the period from the sixteenth century to 1837. Along with registers, the library holds local histories, copies of churchyard gravestone inscriptions, poll books, trade directories, census indexes and a wealth of information about the parishes where our ancestors lived.

Unique indexes include Boyd's Marriage Index with more than 7 million names compiled from 4300 churches between 1538-1837 and the Bernau Index with references to 4.5 million names in Chancery and other court proceedings. Also available are indexes of wills and marriage licences, and of apprentices and masters (1710-1774). Over the years the Society has rescued and made available records discarded by government departments and institutions but of great interest to family historians. These include records from the Bank of England, Trinity House and information on Teachers and Civil Servants.

Boyd's and other unique databases are published on line on **www.origins.com**, on **www.findmypast.com** and on the Society's own website **www.sog.org.uk**. There is free access to these and many other genealogical sites within the Library's Internet suite.

The Society is the ideal place to discover if a family history has already been researched with its huge collection of unique manuscript notes, extensive collections of past research and printed and unpublished family histories. If you expect to be carrying out family history research in the British Isles then membership is very worthwhile although non-members can use the library for a small search fee.

www.sog.org.uk

The Society of Genealogists is an educational charity. It holds study days, lectures, tutorials and evening classes and speakers from the Society regularly speak to groups around the country. The SoG runs workshops demonstrating computer programs of use to family historians. A diary of events and booking forms are available from the Society on 020 7553 3290 or on the website **www.sog.org.uk** .

Members enjoy free access to the Library, certain borrowing rights, free copies of the quarterly *Genealogists Magazine* and various discounts of publications, courses, postal searches along with free access to data on the members' area of our website and each quarter to our data on **www.origins.com**.

More details about the Society can be found on its extensive website at **www.sog.org.uk**

For a free Membership Pack contact the Society at:

14 Charterhouse Buildings,
Goswell Road,
London EC1M 7BA
Telephone 020 7553 3291
Fax 020 7250 1800

The Society is always happy to help with enquiries and the following contacts may be of assistance.

Library & shop hours:

Monday	Closed
Tuesday	10am - 6pm
Wednesday	10am - 6pm
Thursday	10am - 8pm
Friday	Closed
Saturday	10am - 6pm
Sunday	Closed

Contacts:

Membership
Tel: 020 7553 3291
Email: membership@sog.org.uk

Lectures & courses
Tel: 020 7553 3290
Email: events@sog.org.uk

Family history advice line
Tel: 020 7490 8911
See website for availability

SOCIETY OF GENEALOGISTS
The National Library & Education Centre for Family History

Other SoG titles

MY ANCESTOR WAS A...

Royal Marine

KEN DIVALL

INTRODUCTION BY MAJ GENERAL JULIAN THOMPSON

£6.95

MY ANCESTOR WAS...

IN SERVICE

PAMELA HORN

A guide to sources for family historians

£8.50

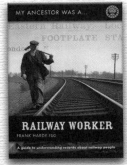

MY ANCESTOR WAS A...

RAILWAY WORKER

FRANK HARDY, FSG

A guide to understanding records about railway people

£7.50

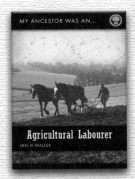

MY ANCESTOR WAS AN...

Agricultural Labourer

IAN H WALLER

Second edition
available soon

MY ANCESTOR WAS A...

COALMINER

DAVID TONKS

A guide to coalminer sources for family historians.
Second edition

£9.50

MY ANCESTOR WAS IN...

The British Army

MICHAEL J. WATTS & CHRISTOPHER T. WATTS

A guide to British Army sources for family historians

£9.99

Order online at: **www.sog.org.uk** or call: 020 7702 5483.
Also available from the Society's bookshop.

14 Charterhouse Buildings, Goswell Road, London EC1M 7BA
Tel: 020 7251 8799 | Fax: 020 7250 1800 | **www.sog.org.uk**

Registered Charity No. 233701. Company limited by guarantee. Registered No. 115703.
Registered office, 14 Charterhouse Buildings, London, EC1M 7BA. Registered in England & Wales